93

THINK HARMONY WITH HORSES

THINK HARMONY
WITH HORSES

An In-depth Study of Horse/Man Relationship

by Ray Hunt

edited by Milly Hunt

cover by S. Baker

This book is dedicated to the man who made it possible—Tom Dorrance; to the horse who made it necessary—"Hondo"; and to the many sincere students whose asking for it made it a reality—with a special thanks to the friends who worked on dull tasks, like tapes and typing!

Table of Contents

Foreword

The name of Ray Hunt is fast becoming a household word throughout the west, Canada and Australia. In years to come when horsemen gather, one of the most familiar sayings will be, "I saw Ray Hunt do this or that with a horse; it's like magic!"

What Ray does is not magic; rather it is common sense. When the Indians first saw the Spaniards riding horses they thought horse and rider were one. That is Ray's theory: to unite the horse and rider into one working unit of both mind and body. He has developed a language that most western people can understand and has become a wonderful teacher, demonstrator and philosopher.

Ray's number one concern is horsemanship and he can develop horses in any stage, from a wild untamed horse to a very delicate show horse. He has learned from experience, with a little help from a few people along the way, but now, as the younger generation may say, "He has it all together—he's cool!"

Ray's influence on the western ranches has been long overdue, as breaking colts was always a drag with absolutely no science, just muscle and guts. Now for many who have followed Ray's theories, it has become an experience everyone can enjoy, one which gives horse and rider a very pleasant feeling at the end of a day.

Thanks to Ray Hunt, horse breaking has become a science that can be enjoyed by professionals as well as amateurs.

Gene Lewis

Introduction

My belief in life is that we can all get along together if we try to understand one another. If you find a friend in life before somebody else finds him you're real lucky. You'll meet a lot of people and have a lot of acquaintances, but as far as having friends—they are very rare and very precious. But every horse you ride can be your friend because you ask this of them. This is real important to me. You can ask the horse to do your thing, but you *ask him*; you offer it to him in a good way. You fix it up and let him find it. You do not make anything happen, no more than you can make a friendship happen.

My goal with the horse is not to beat someone; it's to win within myself. To do the best job I can do and tomorrow try to do better. You will be working on yourself to accomplish this, not on your horse. You will work to recognize how you feel toward your horse and how your horse answers you back; how he understands you, and how he takes it. There shouldn't be any hassle; there shouldn't be a big flareup. Mentally, your horse should not weigh anything. When you ask your horse to do something it should be his idea. This is the goal. In the end, when you ask your horse to do something, he wants to do it, he likes to do it, he understands how to do it, and he does it.

You'll find out when you get this accomplished that you're going to be a horseman. Not that I am one. Someday I hope to be one, but the horse has taught me this. To understand the horse you'll find that you're going to be working on yourself. The horse will give you the answers and he will question you to see if you are sure or not. So it's the confidence you give him and the understanding; the purpose and the meaning behind what you ask him to do that is going to make the big difference. As you work with your horse, see how much of this is the horse's idea, or how much of it is all your idea and if he is forced into it. If he's not forced into it you'll see a great attitude. Your idea should become his idea, and when it does, then there will be no drag.

You will all have different kinds of horses and of course there are all kinds of riders, and this is great. No one is any better than the next one. You are a precious thing in life because you are you—there's no one else in the world like you. That's the same with the horse. He's an individual and this is why I say he's entitled to his thoughts just as you are entitled to yours.

Often a person says, "My horse isn't like that horse." Well, that's good—it would be a shame if all the horses were the same and all the people the same. You try to adjust to fit the situation. One thing we're all working for and trying to learn is to adjust to fit the situation.

I want to respect your thoughts and I'd appreciate it if somebody respected mine. I want to respect my horse's thoughts and feelings. We are the teachers and have to cope with situations as they come up. It can be done. The way to do it is to work on yourself, to recognize and understand the situation. There'll be a lot of questions, and you'll ask what do you do. You make the wrong things difficult and the right things easy as you adjust to fit the situation.

If the rider is alert and aware and in a learning frame of mind, the horse can be the same. The more you deal with your problems, the more determined you are to get something done and the more interesting it is for you to work at it—naturally, the more you're going to learn to respect and understand the horse. It's up to the individual.

A lot of guys say: "How far can I go? How long will it be before I can do this?" I don't know, but you'll know because you're the one that's doing it. You'll know how fast you can go, how much time you've got, how much you're going to work at it. You're going to be honest with yourself and set things up and see. So it's up to each individual.

It's fun for me; of course it might not be to John Doe, but then maybe he's not interested in this kind of a life. If he isn't, well, that's fine too. But you will find out what I'm talking about is a way of life. Only you know how much effort you want to put behind it. How important it is to you to get these things done. If you are satisfied with yourself, you don't have to satisfy me or satisfy John Doe, as far as I'm concerned. If you have satisfied yourself, you are a winner—to me. The only person you have to prove anything to in your life is yourself. I think that a person who doesn't make of himself what he is worthy of is really cheating himself.

I don't know what you have to offer your horse so that your horse can come through for you, but the horse can do anything you ask of him. He can do this to the best of his ability. Some of them can do things better than others, but each one can do his thing his way as well as he can. For me, the horse doesn't have to do my thing my way, but I do want him to do my thing *his* way and like it.

If I had to work for you and I could do your thing my way and like it, this would benefit us both. But, if I had to do your thing your way and I didn't like it, it just wouldn't be me; you'd be wrong in expecting me to stay and I'd be wrong in staying. So again, this is how I want the horse. I just want him to do my thing his way and do it the best that he knows how. If a person is working for me and doing

3

these kinds of things, that's all I can ask of him. It's the same with the horse. Maybe he is not doing it the way we want him to do it, but for him it's the best he can do because that's the way he's made or that's the way he thinks. It's as clear as he can think to do it. That's all you can ask of him. We should know this because we are horsemen and we can feel this. The horse tells you where he is. Work with him on his level. Work him with things he understands. The more horses you can work with, the more horses you can be around, the more different people you can watch and see things happen, the more you learn.

I see people doing things today that I did twenty years ago, and it isn't working any better for them today than it did for me then, but they're still doing it. So again, you can learn something from anyone even if it's to be sure that's not the way you want to do it. I see it happen all the time. You keep watching, then you'll see other things that people are doing that are working for them because they are working for you too. Be observant, then remember and compare. This is true in every walk of life.

You may be doing something you think is unrelated to the horse and it will come to you, and you'll think, "I'll be darned—I'll try that!" So then you try it and there it is—it works. So one little thing falls into line, into place. I wish it would all fall into place right now for you, but it doesn't because it has to become a way of life. It's a way you think. It's a way you live. *You can't make any of this happen*, but you can let it happen by working at it.

It is fun, really fun, because you don't get in a hassle, go into the house at night thinking, "Man, that horse got the best of me. I don't know what to do." It never comes to that. There's never a hassle. You are always working some place the horse understands. You always leave it at that place. It's so much easier on the person and a hundred to one easier on the horse, because the horse is the underdog anyway to most people. But I'll take the horse's part, and

4

I'll prove to you that the horse is right and we are wrong. You will prove it to yourself. As we go along, this is the way it is. We are responsible within ourselves for what happens. Of course you have to get discipline within yourself so that you can have it with your horse. If you don't, this is what will cause your horse to get cranky and take over—get to doing a lot of things wrong. It's because he knows you don't mean what you're talking about because you're not effective with what you're asking him to do. To be effective, teaching must be understood. Be particular within yourself—it doesn't mean a hoot to me but I want it to have some meaning to you so that it will be meaningful to your horse.

I had a fellow tell me one time: "Well, you want your horse afraid of you." I don't want fear. Fear and respect are two different things. Respect you have to have whether it's with a friend or with anyone. If you're going to do some business, why, you have to have respect and understanding or it will fail. You can sing and whistle and be happy getting this respect.

In your own mind you have to have a picture of what you want from the horse, but you are the leader and you can ask him to follow you, just like dancing. It's a rhythm, a harmony—you want your body and his body to become one. This is our goal. It won't always be there in the beginning. Your idea goes across first. It takes some physical pressure naturally, to start with, but you keep doing less and less physical and more and more mental. Pretty soon it's just a feel following a feel, whether it comes today, tomorrow, or next year. You'll never quit learning and I don't believe the horse will either.

I've had different people ask me how long it takes to break a horse. Well, I never rode a broke horse but then maybe I'm a sorry hand. It seems to me that there is a better way of doing things so that the horse gets more sure. He learns something every day; he has to worry less about it;

5

he gets more confidence in himself and in me. It is a learning thing, to me. But as far as "breaking a horse," why, the first time you ride your horse he'll cost you money. The second time you ride him he'll hold his own, but the third day he's on the payroll.

These horses can do it; it's just that simple if you can offer it to the horse. So, it has to come from the rider to the horse. The rider has to make a lot of adjustments so that the horse can understand. Whether you are just starting a horse or working with a more advanced horse, a big key to remember is to always prepare ahead of time. In the boldest print of all, remember the word **THINK**. Be *aware* and *alert, visualize* what you want. Realize you're working with a mind. A lot of people think it's just a horse, but there's a mind operating that horse. This mind gets him doing things because he wants to do them. Or you teach him to do things he doesn't like to do but feels he has to do them anyway.

Sometimes people try to teach a horse to do something he's not really capable of. It's important to recognize how much a horse can do and how much to ask of him. We need to recognize the smallest try, realize the slightest change. Many of us don't know a horse is trying to do something for us until he's already done it.

This is just like a child learning. You want a child to write his name when he goes to school—that's your goal. He's going to write his name as soon as he can. Whether it's the first day or the next month, it doesn't make any difference. First he has to get ready to write—he has to prepare. If the child has never used a pencil, he first has to learn to pick it up, what it means to pick it up, what it feels like. Then he gets to scribbling, making lines; then he begins to make letters of some kind. Later he'll put the letters together. We don't expect the child to write his name the first day or two in school. As soon as he learns to sit down in class and listen to the teacher, he is not immediately expected to write his name. But we expect immediate learning from a horse. We expect him to go from kindergarten to the eighth grade, to high school, and to college without enough time, preparation, or consideration for his thoughts and feelings. We often don't even get him in a learning frame of mind before we begin to *train* him. We don't even have him relaxed and confident, where he can sit down in class and just listen. We skip all that preparation because we are so superior, or neglectful, or lazy. Because we haven't prepared ourselves to recognize the horse's feelings.

We'll ride this horse a few times and we'll kind of get him to turn around today, and tomorrow he's got to turn around better, and better the next day—and he's *got* to do it. The first thing you know he won't do it. I've heard a lot of people say, "My horse was working pretty good yesterday. One time I had him turning around pretty good but now he won't." Well, what they have *done* is that they have *overdone*. The horse was trying to figure them out, but when the rider wanted more and better without even rewarding the horse for what he'd tried to do, the horse said, "This is the wrong thing to do because I get punished for this." So he quits. He bucks them off, or blows up, or freezes up, or rears. Then the rider says, "Oh, gee," and he quits doing what he was doing. The horse is the smart one—he learned how to save his life anyway, whether the rider has learned anything from it or not.

So again you must learn to realize the slightest change, the smallest try that a horse makes. You know and he knows you know. When you feel him start to position himself to turn around or to back up, or whatever, recognize this so you can reward his effort and build on it. Don't make the horse do all the work. He shouldn't have to figure you out and learn to get out of your way to get things done. I don't think anybody should have to get out of anyone's way in life—a horse or a dog or anything else. I think there's a way to communicate. We can learn to understand one another if we listen to one another, if we respect one another's thoughts; we can work on things, figure them out so there doesn't have to be any hassle in life. And again, we will try to do quite a bit of this with other human beings but we won't put up much of a try with a horse.

My goal with the horse is for us to someday be in perfect harmony. It's like a candle light at the end of a long tunnel. It gets brighter and clearer all the time. Even though I realize I will never hold it in my hand, working for this goal is very real and rewarding. Each step along the way is its own reward.

Think Harmony With Horses

An In-depth Study of
Horse/Man Relationship

For several years now I've been traveling around the
country working with groups of riders who are interested
in my philosophy of harmony and getting along together
and wish to build their relationships with their horses on
this foundation. As I approach each new group it's always a
challenge to me. I used to get really bothered and think,
"What am I doing here?" I'll admit there's moments now
when I think about a cattle ranch at the end of a long dirt
road. But I've discovered that the riders tell me where they
are and that's where we begin. The principles are effective
regardless of the age or previous experience of the riders.

It doesn't make any difference if I'm working with a 4-H
group in Idaho, buckaroos in Nevada, or riders on English
tack at a California stable. The horse can be grade to ex-
pensive, registered, "whatever," and it's basically all the
same. I even had a young man in a class once in California
on a mule. He and the mule were excellent material to work
with; the young man tried hard to understand me while the
mule tried hard to understand him. At the end of the clinic
we had a good thing going.

Of course, vocabulary and presentation differ quite a bit
from group to group depending on the age and experience
of the riders, but don't look for a change in philosophy. The

9

aims and goals are constant even if the approach seems to vary.

To digest these goals in the capsule form a person need only know "feel, timing, and balance." But the truth of the matter is that just those three small terms take a lifetime of chewing before they begin to digest. Though I will use them often, I will not attempt to provide the reader with a concrete description of any of them, for to me they are as abstract and elusive as the candle in the tunnel. What "feel" can be to a 4-H child today, with more chewing, each day it will be different. The same is true of a more advanced rider. As the rider grows in awareness and insight, so will the definition of these terms. Each person, in the final analysis, will write his or her own definition day by day. Although I cannot give you "feel," I hope to fix it up to help the reader, or rider, find his own definition.

Impulsion is one of the first things with a horse. If you can't get the horse going for you and have this life when you ask for it, this is a handicap. Or if you can't slow it down when you need to, at the exact instant you need to, this will be in your way. It's like a race car. You're going to go race but the car doesn't run too good. It coughs and misses and cuts out. You are going to go race it anyway but you haven't much of a chance. Your horse is the same way except he thinks and he feels. Your automobile doesn't think and it has no particular feelings toward you or what's going on. But your horse definitely thinks and feels. So again, it's the confidence you give him and the understanding that will make the difference in your relationship with him.

Another basic concept to be aware of in your relationship with the horse is the importance of recognizing where his attention is at all times. There are many indications that will help you learn to recognize this; the most important is to be aware of his ears and eyes. The rider should be alert to these main indications of the horse's attitude, whether approaching the horse and doing ground work or while riding.

Much energy can be lost and a lot of frustration gained by a rider trying to direct a horse's feet in one direction while his eye and his attention are riveted in the opposite direction. It may take quite a lot of effort on the part of the riders to train themselves always to gain the horse's attention before trying to direct the horse. Many common problems in man's relationship with the horse have their roots in the unawareness of the importance of this concept.

When we begin to work as a group, many riders seem surprised that I am very much interested in *the walk*. It's important for me to help the riders realize what is happening at the walk. I want them to begin by walking the horse right out, to be able to control the life in their horse's body through feel.

See if you can bring the life up and get it to really moving free. Your body and your legs come alive. You aren't just sitting there dead on him; you're alive. I want the rider to walk the horse right along—real alive—like they are going someplace. You should feel the rhythm of your horse, feel his attitude.

A walk is a four beat gait and should be regular. You should be able to control it. If you want him to walk a little faster, you reach a little further with your legs, with your fanny, with the soles of your feet and the seat of your britches, with your mind, with your positive thinking. You are picking his feet up and setting them down. You're going with him so he can learn to go with you—feel it. See how little it takes to do the job. If you can put your reins on the horn, fold your arms, and he will do it—that's what you'll do. It's feel, timing, and balance. It can become as natural as breathing.

When you are walking your horse, if you are getting in time with his body and feet you're bringing that life up in his body and slowing it down. Like a radio, you turn the volume up and when you turn it up it comes up NOW, or anyway it should. If not, you start banging on the radio and then it blares your ears and you didn't hear it anyway—so you missed it. This is the way it is a lot of times with the horse. A guy will kick that horse and kick it—pretty soon the horse does go, but it's too late because the cow already went by. Or you're gonna rope one—you kick and kick to get him in position; finally the cow goes by and then something spooks the horse. He jumps out there, but heck, it's too late. Or you go to stop your horse, take ahold of him; he shoots out there and then he stops. It isn't right—life shouldn't be this way. So get your horse ahead of your legs, not dragging you along, running off with you. But you're not kicking and puffing and blowing to get him to walk out, or jog, or move up there. It's like turning the radio up again—you oughta just bring him right up or slow him right down. Just like a swing—you're going to swing it out and your're going to swing it back. When you're swinging it out you won't feel a lot of jerks; it's the same swinging back. It just goes out and back. This is how your horse should be when you get ready to move out. He should move out just as fast as you want him to go and be smooth. When you get ready to bring him back with you he should slow right down the same way. They can do it if we can offer it to them, and they like it, because they get a chance to learn and use their own minds.

To me, we aren't teaching these horses to walk, trot, turn around, stop, or anything. They can do any of these things. What we are trying to teach them is to do these things when we ask them. This is the tough part, to get them to understand to do it *when* we ask. To bring up as much life as we want, to use as little as we want, or to shut it off when we want. The horse can do any of these things if it is his own idea. When we're not on his back he can run out there and stop, turn around, or whatever. When it's his idea it's simple for him and there is no drag. But his problem is to figure out what in the world we want at this particular instant— how much to move out at this time and how much to slow

12

down. The easy way for me to show him is to be a part of him, be right close to him and move with him. When the horse moves and you move with him, your idea and his idea become one. He isn't dragging you and you aren't pushing him along. Again, it is feel, timing, and balance—know what you are doing. You get right down to the horse's feet; you're in time with his body and then he can be close to you and understand what you are talking about. The best place to begin to work for this understanding and communication, to build this foundation, is at the walk.

I try to visualize my body and the horse's body as one. Since my feet do not touch the ground I think of his feet and legs as being mine. When I'm first working with a young horse or attempting to get a new rider to feel this, I will sometimes exaggerate a walking motion. Picture yourself on the ground wanting to move out or to slow down. What do you do to cover more ground? What do you do to slow down?

When you want to move out faster your body livens up, you reach further, you take a longer stride. Or you can use the same amount of energy but not extend your stride—this would give you a more in-place walk.

When you're on the ground and wish to slow down, you don't have to bring the life down choppy and jerky—it comes down smooth. Your body prepares ahead of time. It's this preparation you need to be aware of to make these transitions smooth for the horse.

It's real important that you prepare ahead of time, and this gives your horse a chance to be smooth. When you don't let him know, this is where he can get choppy and unsure of what you want and how you want it. Don't be afraid to overemphasize or exaggerate a movement when you are trying to let your idea become the horse's idea. Exaggeration just makes you more aware of what's taking place. When there is more understanding between you and the horse it will become more natural for you to get these things done, and you will take out the exaggeration.

After horse and rider have been working at the walk for a few minutes I often ask the group to extend the walk with a float in the reins, let him relax, reach out and pet the horse. The horse gets a recess, and I'll ask the riders to rub his neck. Horses seem to kind of like this for some reason—it kind of gets them relaxed and they become a part of you. Maybe they feel like they are important, too. They aren't just a thing that's supposed to please us all the time.

It's real important for me that these horses stay calm. There's a difference, however, between a horse getting soft and a horse getting lazy. If they are lazy, they get dull. Keep up the desire in your horse, a willingness to go someplace and get something done.

After the brief recess, ask your horse for a more collected walk. He keeps right on walking, the nose should come down, the chin should come in a bit. If his nose is out, he just walks into it—into trouble itself. You don't pull on your horse, let him pull on himself. Don't be alarmed if the horse pushes into your hand. You do not pull on him; he pulls on you—there's a big difference. You've got to set an example so he'll have one to follow. When you begin to collect the walk, the nose will come in a little bit, the hindquarters will come right up under and keep walking along; the chin should tuck in a little. Sit tall in your saddle, look out ahead. Look where you are going.

Try to extend the walk again, put some float in the reins and let him move right out and don't doubt him. See how fast he'll walk. This is not a recess—get him to put some effort into it.

If he doesn't understand what you are asking for, he might jog. If he does jog, don't worry and don't worry him; just keep your body in a walking rhythm and ride him through this jog and back into the walk. Don't force him back to the walk; let him find his way back again. By keeping your body in a walking rhythm, even though he

14

jogged, you've made the wrong thing difficult and the right thing easy. You've made it easy for him to walk right out with you. Now try again to see how fast he can walk. Not how fast you think he can walk, but how much energy he can put into a true walk.

If your horse is going to go out again into the jog there is another way you can make this difficult. Make the wrong thing difficult and the right thing easy by picking up on the reins more and letting the horse find his way back to the walk, keeping your body in a live-walking rhythm. This is work on the rider's part. Think! Feel! Let him learn and he will learn to separate what you want.

If you get into a frame of mind where you doubt your horse, you and he are in trouble. If you think he'll jog he won't disappoint you—he'll jog. You are not working on your horse to do any of these things—you need to work on yourself to recognize and analyze what is happening.

Now, see how slow you can walk your horse. Bring the rhythm right down—do not stop—but see how your horse feels back to you when you ask him to slow the life down. Each one of you can learn to do this, fix it up and let the horse find it. This is what you should be doing when you're slowing those feet down, too. You're getting right down to the ground but you're letting him know what it is you want. Think about his feet. The life in his body should be smooth. He should be happy doing this. The rhythm in your body changes to encourage the horse to get in tune with you. When you have slowed the rhythm down, the feet slow down as soft as you can get them, then let the life go out again into an extended walk. Let your horse stretch his neck out there and walk along. You try to keep things where they are not boring for the horse. You do a variety and variation of different things when you are trying to recognize how to understand the horse's movements. You do not get him in the wrong attitude. You do not want him to feel you're boring him, and that what you're asking is monotonous.

15

If I could work with the horse, or with the horse and rider in what I would consider ideal conditions, there would be very little time spent in the arena. But I do work with groups, and if they are going to be within reach of my voice, we stay in an arena. I really try during these sessions to get the riders to understand that all of these things we talk about and work toward can be worked for during the day's normal work, or a pleasure ride away from the stables. There is no reason to stay in the arena and let things become a drill. There are many reasons for not doing just that, but by now I am sure the reader is aware of my feelings about "training" or "drilling." If not, I'm sure to make it clear, since they are both terms I use mainly in the "do not" column.

In the "do" column I look for a kinship attitude between rider and horse. Before the rider even gets into the arena with the horse a very definite relationship has been established. I hope for both the horse and rider's sake that it's one of mutual respect and discipline. Whatever patterns of relating the horse and rider have worked out in the stables will surely carry into the arena.

I was raised on a farm and we had work horses and a few cattle around. We drove horses a lot. My father had a stallion and raised work horses. He was a real good hand with them. His horses weren't afraid of him—Dad had a lot of respect for them and his horses seemed to respect him.

Dad used to tell me: "If your horse will mind you in the barn he'll mind you in the field." It didn't make much sense to me as a boy; I couldn't understand what he was talking about. In fact, it was altogether two different things to me, but as I got older I found out what he meant.

We had a barn that would hold 20 head of horses, 10 on each side, two horses to a stall. You'd go out in the morning, put grain in the manger, and you'd just open the gate and each horse would come into the barn. They'd all go in their own stalls, on their own side—the side they worked on. The halters were left by the mangers and you'd just walk up and put the halters on all of them. They didn't fly back out of there or run off. When you walked up to put the collar on, they stepped back and you put the collar on. The same way, when you walked up with the harness, they stepped over. When you put your hand on them to move away from pressure they just stepped over and you harnessed them up.

Well, like I say, I was raised in this environment and I didn't think it was anything special. But when I got old enough to get away from home, to work for others, I often found things different. Sometimes you could hardly catch the horse after you got him cornered or got him in the barn. Then when you got him tied up, you'd walk up in front of him and he'd probably pull back and then leap right over the top of you. Then you would be trying to put the collar on him and he'd be reaching down in the manger and shoving you down in there too. Now you'd walk up in there to put the harness on him and he'd cow-kick at you as you went by. Finally you'd get out into the field with these horses that didn't have any respect; you'd ask them to pull, and if it got just a little tough, one would fly back and the other would fly ahead. Then he'd fly back and the other would fly ahead. Then they would both balk, and there you were. Man, it sure was good to get back home—I really realized what Dad had. Working these horses that didn't know how to respect you in the barn was hard for them in the field. They got all bothered and excited, and they didn't have to be that way. These were the things I didn't realize until I got away from home.

I am really strict on discipline with my horse and with myself. Before a horse does anything, he gets ready to do it, whether it's walk off, or kick you, or buck you off. He gets ready to do it, but a lot of us don't feel this happening until it's done. If you're going to head anything off, or get things to really coming along fast, you have to be aware of these indications the horse gives out. You need to be aware he's

17

getting ready to move before he moves so you can block it or make use of the movement. If not, he's going to move where he wants. So he has learned to go ahead and move without the person. He knows that you'll kind of come along after he once starts. This isn't what you want but you let him do it. Now you might make him hassle around there trying to get it headed off, but the first thing you know you have quite a drag there with your horse, and in through your horse. He's learned to be this way because he's lived it; you've taught him these things.

You've saddled him up and you've let him walk around and around, eating and grazing. That would be just like trying to teach a kid something in school while he's hopping from one desk to the other eating a lollipop. The teacher is talking and yelling, trying to teach him something. It's a hopeless case, and pretty soon, if you let this go on, the kids would run the teacher out of the classroom. The teacher, or the rider, lets these things happen. These are situations you should never let get out of hand. You do what it takes to head them off before they even start. The horseman needs to be awake, and alive, and alert all the time.

Now we'll assume the riders are all alert and in a learning frame of mind, and that the horses are the same. We have been working to recognize what our horse is telling us of how we feel to him at a walk. We have tried to bring the life up soft and to swing it out with as much energy as we want. We have worked to get his maximum effort in a true walk. We also have worked to recognize how slow and how soft this life can come back down without letting the life die, still keeping some forward movement. Without losing these pictures, pick an object some distance away from you. Visualize a straight line between yourself and this object and try to ride your horse on this line. Try to ride directly to the object. You will probably discover you can't ride him in a straight line. But keep the life coming straight forward through his body. You look where you are going so

18

that the horse knows where he's going. Let him know ahead of time where you're going. See if you can pick a place out there for his feet, and that's where you want him to go.

It's like driving a car. You're not driving right over the radiator cap; you're looking out there a ways so the horse knows where to go. He learns to stay with you. When you ask him to go he just stays between your arms and legs and away you go. Be particular. The horse learns not to be particular unless the rider is.

A lot of you have your business where you have to ride to get your work done and your jobs done. It doesn't take any extra time to do any of these things; it's just getting yourself where you are more aware of it. When you get on your horse start feeling of what's going on, and the next thing you know these things start to fall into place. You just go right on like you're going, but you're giving it a lot more thought. Get in the habit of thinking.

I've worked with some older people in clinics, and some of them said their problem was they had gotten out of the habit of thinking. You know, when a kid's going to school or college, his mind is kept busy, or we hope so. But sometimes when kids get through school they quit digging into new things and reaching for more education. So we kind of get into the habit of not really wondering "why."

I have given a group of people a series of simple math problems. For instance, what is $2 \times 2 + 6 + 8 - 4 + 32$? Some of the group would really try to get the answers. Most of them seemed to wait for somebody else to get it. There will usually be a couple in the group who have worked out the answer but do not have enough confidence in their own thinking to speak up until someone else comes up with the answer. Then they will say: "Well I thought so but I wasn't sure." Some will really work at it and come right out with their answer; but too many of us will just hope somebody else will do it. We expect others to do our thinking for us.

19

This is about what it amounts to in working with the horse. It is: "*Think* what's happening; don't wait for somebody else to tell you." If someone else suggests certain things, that's fine. Try them if you like but don't be afraid to think and analyze and feel what's going on. As soon as you get into the habit of doing these things, it's no different than breathing—you inhale and exhale and you don't have to think about it, you just do it. You get used to getting in time with your horse's feet, and for a while you think, "Wow, this is something else," but the next thing you *know* —you know where every foot is every second, and he knows you know. So, you can get them stopped, or place them, turn them, or whatever. Your timing is right, you're not trying to stop a foot when it's in the air and already going to set down. You'll wait for the next step to direct it or you'll pick up the other foot. Any time you're going to do something with a horse's foot, prepare to do it before it leaves the ground. But after it leaves the ground, you're probably not going to get much done with it without causing the horse to tighten up.

There are lots of opportunities to check yourself out on these things. If the horse doesn't seem to have a clear picture of what you want, try to visualize what you are doing to create this image.

While you're riding, ask for a little longer stride, put a little more effort into walking. Walk from one side of the road to the other, walk from one trail over to the other, walk around this bush this way and that bush that way. Keep your horse's mind occupied. Keep his ears out there looking. Don't let him get centered right around you. Try to keep him moving and looking out. You can get these horses to where the ears are looking right out there because that's where you are looking. That's where he's going with some pride and some energy and effort behind it.

Take him anywhere you want to go—see how little or how much resistance there is. Go across the road, down in the barrow pit, back on the road, or anyplace. To get the horse just to step over I'd be walking on the edge of the pavement and I'd ask him over on the gravel. If he didn't step over except the smallest shift, I just went along and first thing I knew the horse would step over. When the horse does this, just go with him. He might come right back again but this is fine—just come back with him. (You give a little to gain a lot.) Then ask again! They will get so they will just step right over there, especially when you get a breakthrough and get the picture for yourself and the horse.

When I ask for an S pattern with a group, this is what I want them to feel. Feel this horse step over—he'll go a step or two then step back the other way. Feel this foot go over, then the saddle horn goes right over on top of the leg. Go along a little ways and ask him to come out, and first thing you know he steps out and your saddle comes right out over that leg. He steps out. The foot coming out isn't just going straight ahead and the hind end going like you're pushing a wheelbarrow; the front shoulders are reaching out and the hindquarters are staying lined up.

What happens there is: say I'm going to step out to the left so this right foot comes up and I place it a little to the left; so when the left comes off the ground it can really step out.

In other words, I want to step out with the left front foot, so when the right one's coming up I don't set it straight ahead—I set it in to the left but don't shorten the stride. When the right foot's ready to leave the ground I direct it close to where the left one would have been. Then when the left foot comes he's prepared to step out there with it.

If he happens to step straight ahead or a little to the right with the right foot just before you want to ask him to reach the next step left, he's spread out. He'll be out of balance. So you prepare him with the foot *before* you want to ask him to move over. To go to the left you are using your right rein and leg for supporting, closing it off, and your left side is open or leading. The opposite is true in the other direction.

Don't just move your horse over; try to realize what is happening. You should be in rhythm, in time, in harmony with his body. You don't just pry it over, then pry it back. Feel the horse reach out. Don't overemphasize this, but think about it when you are riding. Don't try to make it happen—let it happen. Feel the feet and what they are doing. You're not getting him to cross over. If you're going to want to reach out with your left foot don't neglect to set in the right foot first to prepare for this movement. Fix it up so your horse can find it. This will help your horse.

When you're making an S pattern you're going to be setting a foot in a little bit to get him around that corner, then you'll straighten his body out for a step or two, then you'll be asking for the other side.

When you first begin to do it you may not be making a true S, as this might be overexposing either the horse or the rider. It can be just kind of like a snake would crawl, no sharp curves but weaving back and forth across a straight line. You will visualize a straight line and curving back and forth across it. There are no sharp corners, so there is a spot where the horse is walking straight, more or less, so he can prepare to go the other direction. This straight part is where you want to give the horse a lot of time to make sure he understands you. If not, he'll start to come this way, then just as he starts to come, you'll bring him back and he'll think, "Well, what the heck, why come this way and then I have to just flop right back?" So that's where you let him straighten out and prepare him for a step or two and then ask him to come back the other direction. That's what I want the people to feel—what he does in all these spots. They feel him reach, then they feel him get ready to come back the other way. But don't cut him off—don't chop him off. If you do, he'll get to where there's not a true feel in there.

22

In an S pattern you should be three or four feet from the rail, then six or eight feet away from the rail, then back closer again—if you're using the arena, that is. Which of course isn't necessary. Going along the road or around the brush you're becoming aware of these same movements. I just want the rider to feel what the horse feels and does during these movements. It isn't just walk down there and Yah!—you've done it. I want the rider to realize what he has to do so that the horse can do it. This is the thing behind all the examples I ask the riders to work on.

I don't think particularly equitation or down that line—it's plain Horsemanship, and when you get that going you have equitation because you've got to be balanced on the horse and sitting *right* on him if it's going to come through.

You need to keep your arms lined up, your wrists lined up and then you can do just what it takes to do the job. You're in balance all the way. Your legs and body should be in harmony with his body, not stiff and hard; they are in rhythm with his body. Feel the rhythm.

You're doing a thing together. I use the symbol of "dancing" a lot because there's a rhythm and there are two of you working together and you're feeling of each other. You have ahold of one another and that's the way it is with your horse. You have ahold of him with your legs, hands, and arms, and you're moving with him. The music is the life in your body and in the horse's body. When you are on his back and you move together, this is the rhythm. The life in there that you try to keep going and get your life to blend with. Make sure everything's working together and you're working with it. Feel it. A feel following a feel—there's no pressure mentally or physically. That's what you are offering him.

Think! Feel! Don't forget the recesses; give your horse a break—reach out and rub his neck.

Now walk your horse right along, bring the life up and bring it down real smooth. Bring the life down soft and smooth. Now walk along there for a little, but I want you to slow one foot down (either one) and then stop the next foot. That's how you stop your horse.

A lot of people say, "Well, I want my horse to stop." They want him to slide naturally when they stop him, but they want to skip the basics. They don't realize they should get him to realizing how to slow down first. In the rider's mind, too, there should be a picture of slowing down.

All right—now let's walk ahead again. Think about his feet. Think about slowing one foot down, then stopping the *next* foot. Think what's happening, what you're asking hm to do. This is the part in there where if it's effective, then it was understood. Your hands and your horse's feet should be together so you can slow the feet down and stop them. When you're preparing to stop the live-walking, rhythm in your body stops. You still up and feel out there for him and he starts slowing down. As you're walking along, you're feeling of your horse, and when you're going to stop him you get him to feel through you that there's going to be a change. Then you just slow one foot down and stop the next one.

Have a picture in your mind that you're going to stop a certain foot. If it doesn't stop, there was something wrong in your timing. Your feel and timing are real important. Before a foot leaves the ground you can prepare for it to stop. For instance, if you're going to stop, slow one foot down and stop the next foot. You will slow down the one foot before it leaves the ground and then when the next one leaves the ground you can stop it just as it touches the ground.

Now let your horse go out into an extended walk. See if you can really get the horse relaxed, his head down loose rein. You're just going for a jolly ride. You want your horse to be happy too. Now, if you were going to stop your horse you wouldn't just take hold of the reins real quick and stop him. You'd let him know ahead of time that you were going

24

to stop. So you reach out, you feel of him, then for him, and then you both feel together. This is when you stop. Slow one foot down and stop the last one. You stop that foot just where you want it. Don't change your mind. You've a certain foot in mind that you're going to stop. If it goes on out it is just going to walk right into your hand. But don't force it; fix it up and let him find it. You have to let him know ahead of time. By being consistent, being patient, being aware, there will be fewer problems.

Sometimes when you go to stop your horse you find out your arms and hands are in the wrong place, so you gotta shorten your reins and finally get your hands where you want them on the reins. Then you'll get him stopped, so all this time your horse has learned to push on you because you've taught him to. So when I say "prepare ahead of time," this is one of the things I mean. Let's think about this again a little bit. If a person prepares ahead of time, then he has lots of time to get the job done. But if you wait until the last moment, sometimes it's too late.

Now prepare your horse and go into the trot. The life is going to change; the beat's going to change, so the rhythm in your body changes. The horse feels this change and moves right out underneath your weight. You're the leader and you ask him to move with you. Get ready and lope. There will be a different beat now and you're a part of it. It's a rhythm, a harmony. Your body and his body are one. What we're working on here is controlling the life in the horses's body. Our job is to understand what's going on. Then you can turn the life up or you can turn it down, or you can stop it.

All right—stop at a lope, you're going to bring your horse out of a lope, to a trot, to a walk, then to the stop. You're going to keep him as soft as you can. From the trot you'll slow him down to a walk and then to a stop, see—but it all blends into one.

Sometimes a person will say, "Well, I pull on him, but he

won't stop." The problem there is that it wasn't effective so it wasn't understood. Think about this when you ask your horse to stop.

After your horses are stopped, make sure you give them a little slack so they are rewarded, and when you do take hold of them there's some meaning there. If you don't give your horse slack it's like driving your car with the brake on—you're just going to burn the brake up. First thing you know, when you need the brakes you haven't got them. So make sure you reward your horse by loosening up on the reins so that he can stay light and sensitive to you.

You've got to be awake and alert every minute, every stride, because you're working with something alive that thinks and feels. He makes decisions. If we're not there to help him, he may make a decision we don't want him to make. Then we blame it on the horse. But, I grant you, it's not the horse's fault.

The horse should stay put for you in any gait with a float in the reins. You should be able to control the life with the life in your body. If you've got a little tension on your reins, then you're afraid he's going to go and this encourages him to go because you doubt him. If you give your horse a chance to prove himself usually he won't go. But we have to offer it to him if we're going to get it. Let him go into a trot real easy and see how little it takes to keep him from going into a lope. Just sit quiet in a trotting rhythm. The rhythm in your body sets the pace. You do just what it takes to do the job. Keep the float in the reins and lope—don't do any more than you have to. This is what keeps your horse sensitive and light, is a light contact. If he speeds up, slow him down, then give him slack again—don't just hold him. Horses learn to wait for you. Make sure your body isn't causing the wrong response. Lots of times, if your body gets to hurrying, the horse thinks he's supposed to move up under that life. You're sitting balanced on your horse and there's a harmony; don't let him drop behind your legs. Be aware before he breaks back to a trot—be thinking about it so you can do something about it. Keep your horse even and smooth in whatever gait you both go together. One doesn't go and the other catch up. It's your idea and the horse's idea at the same time. Don't just get on the horse's back and start demanding things of him. To me, when we do this we're real cruel. If we don't let the horse think a little bit too we're not being fair. If our goal is to get the horse to stop, if we teach him how to slow down, I grant you he can get to sliding, but if he doesn't even know how to slow down I don't know how you're going to slide him. But if he learns how to slow down he'll slide and he'll be soft. None of this has to be done in a hurry. Build a solid foundation. Help your horse understand. Again, he can do any of these things—his problem is understanding us.

When you see a horse out in the field or the corral he isn't bothered. There is no worry. He isn't sticking his head up in the air, his ears pointing straight up, and standing there stiff and hard. He's relaxed. This is the mental attitude we want. When you don't have a soft mental attitude you don't ask anything of your horse except to relax and feel back to you, to respond with confidence.

The importance of this is that when we go to speed these horses up and they get tense and bothered, you can take ahold of your horse a little bit and say, "Gee, my friend, don't worry about it—everything's all right." So his neck and his nose will come down a bit; he'll feel away from that pressure and relax.

So then when you speed him up some more, if he starts to get unsure you can say, "Mister, everything is fine." This is our goal, to work these horses where there's no mental buildup, no worry.

See if you can take hold of your reins with just enough pressure, ask your horse to give to you just enough so that you can get him to drop his head down to the ground real relaxed. Now he probably won't know what you want at first so he'll have to hunt for it. He'll maybe try some other things first, but you fix it up and he'll find it.

Your reaction to this may be, "Why in the world would I want my horse's head on the ground?" You probably never would, but this is another example of exaggeration, so that the rider can discover ways to communicate with the horse.

What we'll do here is just hold a little pressure on the reins so he moves his head down and his chin in. It doesn't make any difference if he only responds a little—reward him. If his chin comes in, his head's got to go down. But we'll let him find it. If we use too much pressure it may cause him to back up—just do what it takes to do the job.

Our job in this situation is to get the horse to understand we want him to put his head all the way to the ground. We want him to feel this. We don't want to force it. We'll keep a little pressure there and wait for a change and then we'll reward it. Each time he will become more relaxed and respond by putting his head nearer the ground. But again, we can't do too much or he'll move his feet. If he does move his feet we'll just start over again. The rider will wait as long as it takes for the horse to understand. You'll probably be surprised how soon the horse will relax and respond by putting his head all the way down.

This is the same feel you build everything on. It's the feel you are offering the horse when he speeds up and you're reassuring him by this feel that tells him, "Don't worry—everything's O.K." You have to have lots of patience, and remember: you'll be working on yourself, not on the horse.

You don't have to think of making changes. A person will say: "This would be all right if I could make a change." But you don't change, you just fill in.

I know all of you are riding horses. You're catching them, and getting them saddled up. You are getting on them and going. You're backing them up, you're loping them out, and you're doing everything with them. So it's just in between there somewhere that your horses are not understanding.

You will examine it. Then you will explain it a little closer to the horse, and just go on. It's a short cut in the long run. It's like reading a book, just skipping through and outlining it or knowing the book word by word. If anyone asked you a question about the book you could really answer it. This is what we do with our horses, we really know them so we'll know how to help them understand us.

When we're trying to understand the horse backing up we should try to realize that a horse goes ahead most of his life. Very little time is spent backing except when the horse is in the corral or pasture and another horse jumps at him or bites at him, he may back to get out of the way.

When a horse is going ahead he's pulling with his front end and pushing with his hindquarters. But when we're asking these horses to back up, it's just the opposite. He pulls with his hindquarters and pushes with his front quarters. When he is going ahead the life goes forward through his body. When he backs, the life reverses itself.

So if you crowd the horse into backing, his hindquarters may be pushing because this is what he's used to doing when he moves ahead. At the same time you may have his front quarters trying to move back trying to push the hindquarters out of the way, with the mind a big block of confusion.

Often the rider doesn't realize what is going on and the horse doesn't either. This is the confusing thing. Sometimes the horse can figure it out and get it done. But let's make it a little easier for the horse. You put up just a little feel and let the horse just shift his weight back. Reward him for this try. Then the rider can ask again; this time his feet might move just a little—reward him. This is all he has to do to start with.

When you begin to back the horse you might be thinking "back" but the horse isn't ready to back. You need to change your thoughts and get the horse ready. Prepare the horse to back. To begin to understand backing the horse you'll just ask the horse to shift his weight back. You want him to learn to feel his way off things, not to be afraid to move or afraid not to move.

When you first begin to work for understanding in backing you may want to exaggerate your body movements. Shift the top of your body back so your horse realizes you want to move back, and he will move back under your weight. This is more comfortable for him. As you begin to build effort in backing think of the rhythm. The rhythm is the same as a trot, two feet on the ground and two feet off the ground at exactly the same time—opposite front and hind, except that the life is moving back through the body. Picture this rhythm as it is in the soles of your feet and fanny, your arms and shoulders, and your mind. As you put effort into the back, think of picking each foot up and setting it down, and the horse moving smoothly back under your weight.

If a person was on the ground without the horse and wanted to hurry and back up, the top of the body would tip back, then the feet move underneath. This is the feel I try to have through to my horse. In other words, your horse is an extension of your body. He learns to put effort in backing by the rhythm you have in your body right down to the ground. It becomes his idea so there's no drag. This is what we're working for all the time. Whether we're speeding the horse up, slowing him down, stopping, or backing him, we're working for a feel between rider and horse—less physical and more mental contact all the time.

Tom Dorrance
Tom was raised on a ranch in northeastern Oregon. He gives the
horses credit for his knowledge and awareness of their feelings
and problems. Tom has always been willing to share his attitude,
for he says: "People think they have a horse problem but the horse
has a people problem. I'll be the horse's lawyer and I'll prove to
you the horse is right." And he'll prove it to you every time. Tom
and his wife, Margaret, now live on a ranch near La Grange,
California.

Ray on Hondo with Marie Scovel, presenting the first place trophy for the Hackamore Class at the Cow Palace in 1961. Just nine months before this picture was taken Hondo had been a horse with quite a "people problem." The problems with Hondo caused Ray to seek the "horses' lawyer." Fortunately for horse and horseman Tom had some answers. After a visit from Tom in mid-winter, Hondo was able to win his first competition that spring. He collected several other blues during the season and became a real member of the Hunt family, with the kids riding him, too, before the year was over.

Ray is using Kaweah's Peak to demonstrate during a horsemanship clinic in Fresno, California in the spring of 1976. Many hours in the saddle, more trips back to Tom, and much "going to bed thinking about it and getting up thinking about it" created a picture of understanding and harmony between horse and rider. Ray is showing that the use of the reins isn't necessary when horse and rider become one.

Sometimes it's difficult for a rider to realize the importance of the walk. Ray emphasizes that the basic skills in communication between horse and rider are developed in the walk.

This informal lineup was snapped in a "paddock" at Macksville, New South Wales, Australia during April 1978, while the Hunts were guests of John Stanton. John's horse facilities in Macksville saw many such groups as John introduced Ray to Australia and his Australian "mates" to Ray. On one occasion it was almost a crowd with 43 people for noon "tea." Left to right: Devon White, Maurice O'Niel, John Stanton, Ray Hunt, Dick Adams, Tom Stanton, Bruce McNaughton.

Here Ray and Kaweah's Sugar create a picture of unity as they go into a curve at the lope. Around our corral we'd use the term "right on." The horse's feet and legs are in time and his head is hanging straight up and down.

Many things can be accomplished while walking along a road edge. Here Ray has "Right On Doc" moving out well. The horse is looking where he is going and things are uniform (in balance).

At a clinic on the Holland Ranch near Dillon, Montana Ray is demonstrating teaching a horse to trailer load. The horse belongs to Verne and Chad Holland. The gelding was raised on the ranch and this week's colt class was his first experience with all the things he'll be expected to do for his owners. When this picture was taken the horse had been introduced to the trailer about 30 minutes before and had been loaded and unloaded several times. Here you see the colt let down and relaxed. He's looking into the trailer and loading without pressure.

This picture didn't take in quite all of the group of enthusiastic students who came to Spring Creek, Nevada in October 1977. They came from Canada, all the Western states, and as far away as Nebraska and Minnesota to meet the teacher's teacher. This special clinic held at the Horse Palace in Spring Creek near Elko, Nevada, was a first. Both Tom and Ray worked to share their ideas with the group who showed their sincere interest by coming so far and working so hard. It is hoped it will become an annual affair.

Charlie Van Norman of Tuscorora, Nevada, at Spring Creek during the 1977 Dorrance-Hunt Clinic. Charlie is a long-time resident of Elko County, Nevada. He is a successful rancher and an accomplished horseman. He was a real asset to the class, with his sincere questions and eager mind. He came to learn, and he helped displace the myth of the western ranch culture that youth and strength are the prime requirements for breaking a horse. There is a lot of value for the horse and horseman in experience, wisdom, and an ageless learning attitude.

Conclusion

Your horse should feel under you just like you could lead him out from under you and you'd go ahead and do your thing. You shouldn't have to hold him in here and ride him up there.

To start with, you will have to do this with a colt because he doesn't know how to move out. He stays behind your legs, or he's going too fast—he's going faster than your body. So you get him to move up or stay back. As time goes on it's like taking a flat piece of clay and working it up here and wadding it up there—the first thing you know your way of movement is his way of movement and you are one. But you have to feel it. It's like dancing, which is an expression I use a lot. It's a harmony, a rhythm. You're not fighting it—you're enjoying it, there is no drag. When you're dancing, the man usually takes the lead, but you're not dragging your partner. It's right there; you are taking the lead but it's just a little bit ahead so this other body can follow you. It isn't a drag. This is the way it is with your horse; you're taking the lead but you're not dragging him. Yet he's not taking over and taking you. It's one body and one mind, but you have the say. As soon as you get aware of this and feel this, you'll know this is the way it is all the way through. Whether you are stopping your horse, or backing him, or spinning him. It's rhythm, and the better you catch the rhythm, the better horseman you're going to be. Feel the rhythm and the harmony.

Your horse learns that he can do anything you want him to do and he's glad to do it; he's ready to do it. You have set it up for him. You've never discouraged him, you've never belittled him, you've really bragged on him and his good qualities. When he did something wrong you didn't make a big thing of it. You went along with him there, too, and showed him that wasn't too good a thing to do—yet you didn't criticize him or hammer on him. So, as time goes on from day to day, week to week, month to month, and year to year, I'll grant you that you can build a friendship and something that's unbelievable. Again, these horses are more sensitive than we can ever imagine. As we go along you'll see how sensitive they are. You develop this sensitivity. Let them use their keenness to show how sensitive they are—to teach us.

They can buck us off, and run over us too, and we'll think, "Yah! He's sensitive all right!" But he still is, you know, it's US who made the mistake. We're the humans, we're supposed to be the smartest.

Again it's funny, it's comical. I've had a lot of laughs with different things that happen, but gosh, at the time the horse, he was just saving his life. Or so it seemed to him. A lot of times the horse is so much smarter than we are that he'd do a lot of things if we'd just get out of his way.

It's not a thing you worry about—it's an individual thing. What each gets done depends on how important it is to the person. Some people are very limited in time; they have other jobs and other responsibilities, but they will accomplish a lot more with their horse in a shorter time this way. But you won't worry about the horse getting the best of you because you won't look at it that way. When you've got the horse to where he doesn't worry either, you've got a better chance of teaching him something. Just like you have a better chance of teaching your boy or girl something, or learning something yourself, if you don't get bothered.

If you're unsure or worried your horse senses this; he feels it. He feels this unsureness in there and maybe he will really get unsure of some things himself. You telegraph right down through your body: "Man, that doesn't feel good at all." Your more sensitive horses will get to where it's just this unsureness in there that keeps them from doing what you want. So then if you force them, they're liable to buck with you, and you can't stand that because you're not sure you can ride him. So you go around that knot, you don't untie it, so he's learned right there how not to try, and you have him on the road to disobedience. First thing you know, he's got you right in his pocket. By the time you want him, there's nothing true or dependable in your relationship. You haven't got a friendship—it's just kind of an acquaintance. It might be and it might not. When you need him he doesn't need you and vice versa. But this other way, there's never a doubt; when you ask him to do something, it's not a kidding sort or joking sort of thing. If you ask him to do something, he knows you mean it and that there is a reason why you ask him. So he does it because he is your friend and you're his friend and you have taught him this. You have built this kind of relationship. You have let him learn it because you've gone with him when he was discouraged, disappointed, worried, and bothered. You've accepted it and you've shown him a softer way. He didn't have to do anything in particular other than just not worry. So the horse learns that "Boy, you're all right." Horses get to where they'll do anything they can for you, but they know that you will for them too.

A lot of people say, "Well, you can't show a horse down the road every day that way." To me, that's the only way you can—or the only way I'd want to go with a horse. If the horse has to go down the road and show for you every day, scared of what you're going to do—going to get a spur run through him or his head jerked off—why, he isn't going to last long. He can't last long because of the mental pressure. I say he can't, but there are individuals who might. However, it's tough because he's afraid of what's going to happen, what's going to hurt. He might last for a year or two but he doesn't quit because he's an old horse—maybe he's only eight or nine years or even younger—it's because he's already blown up. He's given up. A lot of horses quit and give up before that if you can't consider their feelings. But this way, they'll do what they can. If they don't win, that's all right; they'll do their best. They won't feel the same for each performance any more than you will. There are some days when you feel like you can take the world on; there are other days you're not even going to try it. Your horse is the same way—there are times when it just doesn't take anything for him to do it—it was great. Then there'll be other times when it just doesn't go right. He just doesn't feel right and things won't go well that day. So he didn't win that show, and maybe he didn't even place. It's all right—go on to the next one, if you want, but don't be upset with your horse.

I'm sure you've played games in sports when you were the same way. Playing basketball or football, there were days when, boy, things would set up right for you and you could do no wrong; there were other days, man, you wished you had stayed home.

Again, working with these horses we set the example and try to build a friendship, and we can. It's easy to do it with the horse. But you have to work to understand him, understand his problems, understand his qualities, whether you think they are good or bad or whatever. They are all good. So you don't try to change anything with the horse—you just build on. He can usually do the things we ask him to do—the trouble he has is communicating with us. Communication, again, is adjusting to fit the situation.

If you are going to sell someone a bill of goods and you

know that it's good for him, you'll get it done if you're a good salesman. But if you're not, you won't be a salesman very long because your boss will have somebody else in there doing your job. It's the same way with the horse. If you're going to get the horse to step around behind, or to step around in front, or to back up, or to lope out, or to collect up—then you're going to get it across to him so that he understands what you're talking about, and he likes it.

Now there are a lot of horses doing things that they don't like doing, but they are the victims—they have to do them. This is what I don't like to see in a horse. I don't like to see a horse doing things that are our ideas but not his. I believe the horse can do these things we're asking him to do and really want to do them. So you don't make anything happen. You let things happen. If you let him do it, he likes it and then it's his idea; but to do this well you're going to have to be a teacher! You're going to have to understand the horse's feelings. You will work on yourself more than on the horse to realize what is taking place.

I've never been a teacher in a classroom but I don't think the teachers are going to make their kids do anything. I don't think that when students walk into the classroom the teacher meets them with a club and says: "Now, kids, we're going to *do this*!" A good teacher not only does not need a club but doesn't even have a "have to do this" mental attitude. He knows how to approach the student and present the material so that the student is eager to learn. He can fix it up for the student and let him find it. Of course, not all teachers have the same gift for teaching. I've heard so many people say: "My child really got a good start in school; he had a good teacher," while another one will say: "I wish mine had gotten a good start; he had a poor teacher." Now, I don't know whether these children had good teachers and a good start or bad teachers and a bad start. Both things can happen to a child. It can happen to a horse. But, if a child or a horse is having problems it's so easy to just say: "Augh,

41

he's slow, he just doesn't understand." So the thinking is to just go ahead and work with the fast ones and let the others hassle along. Don't give any time or thought to the ones with the poor start. But maybe the other children weren't smarter but just caught on sooner because they were less bothered, whereas the slow student was maybe just as bright, but his personality or characteristics, or the situation he was under made things more difficult for him. Perhaps he was bashful, shy, or didn't have the confidence he needed in that teacher to get a good start. But, to a real teacher, all the students are equal. This child, the one who is having some trouble learning or behaving, gets special care from a good teacher. This doesn't mean keeping him after school. The teacher won't even make an issue of it at all. But you'll see the teacher, maybe, stop by the desk and encourage the child, help him a little bit. Then the teacher will help the others. You won't see the teacher doing much for those who don't need much help, but there will be a real good friendship with them anyway. A good teacher is able to encourage all students to develop their abilities. All students are different, and so are all horses. A lot of times you will present something to the person, or the horse, and they will do plumb opposite of what you want. But the way you presented it was without understanding.

Let's get back to teaching the horse and ways of making him understand. Maybe by presenting what you want in a different way you'll get a different try—you'll get understanding. I'd say that about 99% of the time the horse isn't doing what we would like him to do is not because he's trying to get the best of us. It's because he has no choice. The way we present it, it just doesn't come through that way to him. You'll be the one who analyzes how he reacts and you'll realize he doesn't know what you want—he doesn't understand. We have to present it to him in a way he does understand, but you can see that we have to be the teachers. We have to be the ones who really make most of the adjustments. Sometimes we make a 90% adjustment just to get the horse to make a 10% adjustment. But after a while we'll ask him to do it and it will happen. It will be one mind and one body because his idea will be your idea, any time you ask for it. He will have learned it because you have offered it in an understanding way. You've made it enjoyable for your horse to learn. You've worked on the level he understands. You've kept his mind right and let him know ahead of time what you wanted so he doesn't have to become bothered. Make it a way of life with the horse to be the way you want—listen and learn. You listen to your horse and learn from him.

Questions and Answers

1. *How do you teach a horse to back?*

You fix it up and let him find it. You make it difficult for him to stand there but easy to move his feet. Just pick up on your reins and wait right there. All you want is for the horse to get ready. The saddle horn will start to move as soon as the horse starts to move to release some pressure. Reward him. At this stage, I don't care if the horse moves his feet or not, just get him prepared to back. It becomes the horse's idea. He gets ready and then he can go; first thing you know he'll start carrying it further and further. It gets to where it doesn't weigh anything. Sometimes when I am first working with a young horse who doesn't know yet what I mean, I may exaggerate some things. When I go to back my horse I might lean back, really lean back. This will cause him to shift his weight back in order to feel comfortable or balanced. He might need these things over-exaggerated in order to get the idea of what we want. You may have to over-exaggerate a lot of things sometimes to get the point across, even as over-exaggeration is used in a child's learning process. You exaggerate it but as they start to learn you take the exaggeration out and leave the true thing in there. He's learned to follow a feel but you have to let him learn it. Now, see how little it takes just to get him ready. You're adjusting to get the situation all this time.

Remember that when you're backing the horse is backing between your legs. Your legs are backing up in rhythm with his legs. His feet are in your hands, which are picking up each front foot as it's ready to leave the ground. In other words, it's a guideline. Your weight is back, your life is back, the desire in your body is back, and his is too.

2. How do you keep a horse from throwing his head while backing?

All you do is hold your hands still. When you go to back him up you've got some pressure on somewhere, mentally or physically, or both, that's causing him to throw his head. He doesn't understand it—it bothers him. He doesn't understand what you want. So all you do is take ahold of the reins; hold on to them. Put enough pressure there so he can move away from it but do not pull on him—fix it up for him to find. Keep your arms and hands fixed right there so if he throws his head he bumps himself. Don't let him work your arms like a yo-yo.

You're trying to do several things at once. You're trying to get him so he doesn't get worried when you take hold of him—plus you don't want him to throw his head—plus you'd like for him to try to back up with a decent attitude.

3. How do you take care of the bad habits?

He has to start doing something, then he does it, and pretty quick it's a habit. He has to get started first, so when he's beginning to do it he has some idle time and things to think about besides what you want him to think about. If you would make what he is learning a little more interesting for him, he wouldn't have idle time—then he'd never get to forming bad habits.

Once he gets to doing something, then he learns what he lives, so then it's a habit. When you go to break a bad habit, it's usually calloused quite a bit so it takes a lot of thinking and lots of work on your part from one second to another. You want to get him over it in a day but he didn't get that way in one day. Ride your horse with more awareness of what's taking place or what hasn't taken place so you can start getting things to happen for the better.

4. *How do you start a horse?*

It's not cut and dried how I start a horse—there's no particular thing I do. I don't know what I'm going to do until I approach the horse; then he tells me what he needs and what I have to do to get him to accept me. There's no way I can tell you what I'll do because I don't know what the horse is going to tell me I have to do. These are the things I want you to visualize for yourselves so you can picture what's happening. You will realize you have to adjust to fit the situation. It's all different, yet it's all the same.

5. *What do you do about a horse jigging on the way home?*

If I answered all the questions with "adjust to fit the situation" there would probably be less chance of any rider misunderstanding or misusing what ideas I present in answer to the various questions. There would be many ways to answer! *But many questions to ask.*

Is the horse in question a colt with an inexperienced rider? Is it an older horse with a firmly established pattern of behaving? All the whos, whats, and wheres determine the

47

whys, whens, and hows. Is the horse someone's hobby? A horse to stall and feed generously and ride once a week for *the owner's* pleasure, with unawareness of what might be boring to the horse? Is the horse a colt someone is "training" and the rider wants to get his time in on this horse to get going on the next horse? I mention these kinds of things because I would need to know the exact situation to really answer the question. However, I can give you some ideas to try.

Take the horse in a little circle, and when you get to the certain spot in that circle where the horse doesn't weigh anything, then you start towards home again. If the horse starts jigging again, you make it difficult for him by going back to the small circles in the other direction. Set it up for him to feel for the soft place, and when you start for home see if he will carry this feel.

If the horse is having difficulty responding, you might try putting him in more of a bind. He may walk along sideways in a bind for a bit but this is difficult for the horse and he will look for an easier way. When you feel the horse's body soften, ease up. You've made the wrong thing difficult and the right thing easy.

Also, consider the answer to "How do you discourage a horse from jogging when you want to walk?" Some of that material may help you solve your problem.

6. *How do you discourage a horse from jogging when you want to walk?*

One reason a horse won't walk is because the person isn't getting him to get down on the ground and lengthen his stride. Usually, for a horse to get out and walk, really walk, he should be relaxed. But many horses aren't relaxed when they walk—they are tense and tight. In this frame of mind a horse will walk a little ways and then he'll go into the trot, or a dead jog. All you have to do there is discourage the jog, make it difficult for him to jog and easy for him to walk. As you're walking along and he starts to jog, keep your body in a live walking rhythm. Your arms and hands stay the same, too. As he goes to jog, the horse's feet may go "bump-bump-bump" into the rider's hands, instead of the nice "together" feel. So the horse will usually come back and find that rhythm with the rider's body and hands. The place where it felt good. You may have had to exaggerate this but the next thing you know he feels the rhythm and doesn't want to jog. The horse wants to follow the rider's feel and stay where it's comfortable in this nice stride. You made it just a little difficult and *let* him learn not to do it. You don't *make* him not do it. Then he would have a different attitude. Maybe he wouldn't want to learn. Always make it easy for your horse to learn!

7. *How do you get a horse to carry a soft feel into the trot?*

He should roll right out in a trot. The life should come up smooth. It shouldn't come up with a jerk. Be a part of him, roll with him.

At first it doesn't have to carry. There is a difference between a horse giving and carrying. One horse may kind of understand how to carry and he'll get his nose down and give you this soft feel as long as you ask for it. If your horse will do this, it's fine. But if he doesn't, don't worry. If he'll just give to you a second, reward him. Give him some slack and then ask again a little later on. It won't be long until he'll just put his head down there and carry it and be real soft. But you have to offer it to him. Your hands stay soft too; they aren't demanding, they are soft and pliable.

Sometimes when a rider asks for this feel he reaches out there for the horse, but the horse tightens up instead of softening. He should soften, his head should come down a little—the nose comes in a little bit and the horse gives to the rider. The horse responds by turning loose to the rider. He's in a neutral feel. When your horse is in neutral, then you can take him anywhere you want to take him.

8. *What can you do about a horse that wants to keep moving when you want him to stand?*

If a horse is willing to move, make use of it. Don't discourage the horse when he moves. A lot of people will keep after him, keep setting him back on his tail and getting after him to stand still. Some day you're going to want this horse to get handy; to do this he'll have to move. So make use of every move; don't discourage his moving.

When he's moving, start putting his feet around in a circle someplace, picking his feet up and setting them down. Get in time with his body and put all this energy to work for you. While he's moving and you're making use of it, first thing you know this will get kind of old and the horse will stop relaxed. When he does, reward him by putting a lot of slack in the reins and sitting quiet. You've fixed it up and let the horse find it.

But if you use the other attitude that you're just going to "make him stop," when you want to use this life you may have some fear or tension built in. He may be afraid to go because you're going to "make him stop." Let the horse teach you what to do.

9. *If you are riding in a corral or arena with an open gate and the horse wants to go out the gate, how do you handle it?*

If you anticipate he's going to test you on the gate, you

50

might do a little more with your inside leg at this stage. You'll do a little more with that hand, too. You might not be taking hold of the rein firmer but you'll do enough to get that eye, to get his attention away from the gate. You'll be doing something on the side away from the gate to get his mind off the gate. Get him hooked onto your hand and leg on the inside.

In the arena, when the horse is coming around toward the gate, his body is round but when he shapes up to go out the gate it straightens out. The hindquarters have moved in a little, pushing the shoulder toward the gate.

Sometimes the rider's reaction is to use the outside leg to bump the horse away from the gate. However, this can cause the horse to just lean on that leg. The attention is already in that direction, so if you do too much with the outside leg it just draws the horse more that way. So, if you are working on the outside shoulder it's liable to make the problem worse. You'll do very little with your outside leg but it will be in there blocking him. If you use your inside leg back towards the hindquarters it will help the life in the hindquarters to swing on through there. Instead of bracing the other way and shoving you out the gate, the life comes on around.

Try to keep an arc in his body so the horse won't get solid between his shoulder and his hip. His rib cage won't get tight along there pushing to the outside. You'll use the inside rein to keep his head straight and his shoulder in. As a foot starts off the ground be alert to pick it up and set it in.

When you're coming towards the gate and the horse starts to lean on the rider to go out the gate, this spot won't feel good to the horse or the rider. This is probably not the only place this problem shows up. When you're riding down the road or anywhere, stay alert to keep the horse between your arms and legs and with your feel. Then when you come by this gate he will stay in this feel rather than to lean on you and push to get out the gate.

51

Other times you will purposely set it up to let the horse go out the gate, and you'll go with him. Ride him through the gate, around the gate, and by the gate. Pretty quick he should get so he doesn't weigh anything. There will be a spot in there just as he goes out the gate that he doesn't weigh anything. You and the horse are one. That's what you want going around by the gate so you'll work that in with coming by the gate. The spot will feel as good to the horse as it does to you. That feel of staying together is what you're trying to establish. In this instance you're going with him so he can stay with you.

10. *How do you get a horse to go away from the barn?*

You wouldn't try to take him away from the barn; you'd just make it difficult for him to hang around there. You would make it difficult by not letting his feet stop—just keep his feet moving.

You don't pull or jerk on him; just make it difficult for him to stop. Pretty soon he will start to leave the barn area and when he does you go with him. Reward his try by making this comfortable. If he turns to come back, why just come with him, but don't let him park—just keep his feet moving and he'll find his way out away from the barn again. Each time he'll get farther away from the barn. He'll get so he'd just as soon be out away from the barn as he would to be there at the barn. You've made the wrong thing difficult and the right thing easy.

11. *How do you want a horse to stop?*

When your horse stops right for you and it feels real good, if you stop to think about it, the reason he did was because he felt good right down to the ground. Your timing to the ground with his feet was the whole thing to him. It felt good to him so he could feel back to you. You were letting him know ahead of time by your body rhythm stilling up that you wanted him to stop.

The stop you'd want to feel is with the weight back on the hindquarters, the way a horse would feel coming down a hill (at a walk, trot, or lope)—when he feels good to you. His weight is shifted back. He's balanced back on his hindquarters. It's your feel and timing working his hindquarters up under him. It feels good that the weight is back down through his hindquarters and his back legs. Hold the hindquarters up under him and keep them coming. You'll be lightening up the front end. Another question was asked about keeping a horse from getting light in front. Well, you would want him light in front with the weight tipped back on his hindquarters, the hindquarters working under him.

You wouldn't ask him to put effort into stopping. You'd ask him to prepare to stop. Then you can ask him to put effort into the stop when he's learned to keep balanced right.

12. *When should you start getting a horse used to a rope—for instance swinging the rope?*

You could start getting him used to a rope when you first approach him. It depends on the horse—how he takes it, what his attitude is towards the rope. He could be getting used to the rope when he's getting used to you, or the blanket or the saddle.

It depends on how important it is for you to get him used to the rope. If you're not ever going to use a rope on him, well, it isn't too important to get him used to it. But if you're getting a horse ready to rope on or to use on a ranch, then the first time you ride him you can get the rope down and rub him with it, pet him with it and get him used to it. But then, there are some horses that may not be ready for this. You'd be overexposing them quite a bit. So your better judgment will tell you how much to do. It's no different than when you go to get on one. When he's ready to get on for the first time, you get on him. When he's ready to accept the rope you'll keep exposing him to it and the first thing you know it's no different than any of the other things he's gotten acquainted with.

You always make it easy on the horse and keep him in a relaxed and learning frame of mind.

The sooner you can get him used to it the better. It's like the slicker—getting your horse used to the slicker. You'll get him used to the slicker the first time or two you're on his back. That's the time for him to get used to it so it's not something new later. You might want to put your slicker on someday when it's raining. If you wait until that day to introduce it to the horse you may have trouble. Your rope is no different.

13. *When a horse starts to come (or give), do you ease up on him?*

You've heard me speak of feel, timing and balance. You've heard me say—you feel of your horse, you feel for your horse, then you both feel together. Now when you feel of your horse, it's how does he feel? Where is his attention? Is he tight? Is he relaxed? Is he lazy? Is he alive, alert, happy? There are lots of questions when you *feel of your horse.* So, then you feel for him. You're asking him to feel back to you with a softness. Now it depends on what you felt first *of him,* what you will ask when you feel *for him.*

When you felt of him it told you (again) what you're going to do when you feel for him. Whether you're going to get a little bit, a try, or you're going to get some changes.

54

His attitude tells you what you're going to feel for and how much you're going to ask for. Then when *you both feel together* is when he responds to what you were asking him to do, whether it was to get his attention, to slow his feet down or to move his feet up. It doesn't make any difference. It's in the rider's mind what he was asking the horse to do. The rider needs to recognize and realize when the horse does feel with you and you both feel together. Now how long you'll carry this depends, again, on how far along your horse is—how he understands when you feel for him.

Of him is one thing; for him is something else. When you're feeling of him you're feeling how he's operating— what his thoughts are on your thoughts when you ask for him. So you will know what to do when you ask for him by how he responds to you.

I don't know what you are going to be asking him to do, but your wish is for him to turn loose and give to you, whether it's stopping, turning around or going ahead.

It's your idea and his idea becoming the same idea at the same time. When you both feel together, that's the balance—feel, timing and balance.

14. *How can I get the horse's attention more?*

As a rule a person has his horse's attention way too much, but it's in a bothered frame of mind. The horse is aware that you're there. I'm sure the question is, "How can I get him to respond the way I want?" You want the horse to get ready to respond to you. The main thing is not to have him bothered. If you're riding your horse down the road, out in the field or wherever and his attention seems to be on something other than where you want it, see if you can draw it back to you for an instant and then let it go again. By doing this you will be able to gain and hold his attention.

55

For instance, if your horse is looking off at something to the right, maybe you'll move your left leg a little and touch the left rein more, and his attention will change—that's fine. Let his attention go back again to wherever it might be, then see if you can draw it back again, but see how little it takes. Let him find it. It's amazing how sensitive the horse is. If you get to doing too much then you'll upset him. When the attention changes, settle for that—then let it go back again.

Whatever way the horse's attention is directed, if you want to change it use the opposite leg and hand. Just try wiggling the leg a little—maybe just reach out with your hand a little on your rein and see if his attention changes. This will prepare him so that later on when you go to turn around, or stop, or whatever you want to do, when you reach for him he feels right back to you and you get his attention off some other thing out there. But he shouldn't get bothered. His attention should come to you but not with a bothered frame of mind like "Oh, gee whiz, now things are going to happen!" It shouldn't be that sort of an attitude.

The attitude should be that he's ready to respond to whatever you want him to do. So you are careful of how you get his attention. His attention and his attitude of responding back to you should be a "live softness."

This gets back to: you feel of him, you feel for him, then you both feel together, even if it's just getting his attention back with you as you are going down the road. It doesn't have to be doing any particular thing just being ready to respond to whatever you're going to ask him to do. In other words, it's respond and respect. When you reach for your horse he responds with respect. Respect is understanding, not fear. When you reach for him he should respond with respect. There will be times when your horse will respond but the respect isn't there. What I mean by this is he recognized your effort to gain his attention but he's still looking off some other place. He isn't responding with respect. This is what you want to try to avoid. Maybe he is ready (in position) to come on his feet, but he's not ready to come with his mind. You'll go along with him a little ways there until you get his mind ready—until his attention comes to you—then he'll respond on the feet. He'll do whatever you are wanting. It's respond and respect.

15. *What do you do about a horse you have to hold all the time?*

The horse you're talking about seems like he's moving into pressure all the time. If I've got the question right, you're asking about a horse you have to hold all the time. I take it that it's a horse wanting to push ahead, crowding. If you're not holding him back he'll speed up in any gait.

You slow him down and release him again, but don't hold him. The more you hold him the more he'll expect to be held and the harder or more you'll have to hold him.

The life in his body is pushing on you so you just hold until it quits pushing, then you release. He'll probably move up again but then he just moves into pressure again, and then when he releases (or softens), you release. In other words, he is the one that quits pushing. He's pulling on you; you aren't pulling him. But don't hold him and he'll get so he'll stay put and wait.

But as far as "holding your horses," you should be holding him to the extent that it's your idea to ask him to move, when you ask and as much as you ask. So you are really always holding him, but it's with a feel and not with a lot of pressure on the reins, like it might sound. When you're holding something, it's ready to move at your wish or your desire.

16. *What can the rider do about a horse walking with his head off to one side?*

If he walks with his head to one side, there's something sidetracking him so the life is going through his body crooked. So use the opposite rein and the opposite leg a little and you should see a change in his expression. For instance, if he is walking with his head a little to the right, you'll probably feel his hindquarters are leaning a little to the left. Do a little more with your left rein and your left leg and you ought to feel his attention come to the left and his hindquarters straighten up (or even go a little bit to the right). By offering this to the horse, the first thing you know he'll get the life coming straight through his body. It's something the rider has to feel. The rider has to recognize it to be able to correct the problem. It isn't a big thing you do. It's the little things that make the big difference. Remember to *let* him find it; you don't make him find it. Settle for the smallest change and the slightest try; first thing you know it will become meaningful to him. He'll get the life straight through his body and get lined up to where the life is equal on both sides.

To start with, you might exaggerate, get him to looking more often the opposite of the way he's had the habit of carrying his head. You can get it straightened out if you'll recognize and reward the slightest try and smallest change. Be careful not to make an issue of the problem. Don't upset the horse; just offer it to him and let him find it.

17. *If a horse speeds up and you offer him a feel to slow down, but he's hard, what can you do?*

It depends on the horse, its attitude. There are different things you would do. You might take one rein a little shorter than the other to put him in a bind; his "way out" would be for the feet to slow down.

Also, see how much distance you can work in at a walk—don't hold him. Distance is the float in the rein so when you reach for him and the slack starts to come out of the rein he starts to respond. If when you reach for him he just keeps going, you'll just wait until you feel a change come. He might not slow right down but you'll feel him kind of turn loose. Reward him by putting some slack in, then set it up again. The meaning will start to take hold and he'll understand. Do this at a walk, then you can build it in more at the trot, then speed up.

But if he doesn't respond properly at a walk or a trot it's pretty tough on him to respond properly when he is speed up. It's more apt to get out of control and get worse because you've got more speed going—more of a bothered attitude, if you're not careful. The faster you go the more a horse can get bothered as he speeds up, but most horses will because the rider doesn't kind of understand the feel—the difference between soft liveness (aliveness) and the tightness and tenseness. The horse should just liven up but not get hard and tense.

A lot of times the faster a horse goes the tighter he gets; so if you'll get your horse to where he'll respond at a walk and trot it's easier for him to respond speed up. This is something you build into your horse when you're first starting him, first riding him. You should be aware of this so that you don't have to correct it later on.

If you are trying to correct a problem, another way to approach it would be to try to get him in neutral and work from there. Neutral would be where he'd just turn loose. He might not give, but he'd turn loose. Turn loose means when you reach for him he softens. His feet might still be going, but you'll pick up a soft feel. The horse will tuck his chin a little bit and kind of turn loose—then you're prepared to get down to his feet. Between that loose feel and

59

the hardness that you have he'll learn to get into kind of a neutral place. Then when you add a little bit you'll start getting to his feet if you'll wait and let him find it.

As his feet start to slow down then you can release him and let it go again. When he once gets the message he'll turn loose and come down soft. He'll turn loose and give at the same time. Then you'll build effort on it later. You don't try to get effort on it while you're trying to get him to understand how to turn loose and give. It's like anything else—you learn how to do it, then you learn how fast or how good you can do it. You don't try to get that before you get understanding.

It has to be effective if it's going to be understood, so you have to do what it takes to do the job. I can't tell you how much pressure you use. It's recognizing a change—you have to feel a change come and when you feel a change the horse feels you feel it, so he starts understanding. It's respond and respect, but the person has to feel it, has to recognize it.

Now a lot of times the horse doesn't understand what we mean by what we're doing. In other words, the horse doesn't know how to operate from what we're thinking about. He doesn't know how to operate from this softness. You might be offering it to him, but he has never operated from there before. He's only known hardness and tightness, but if you understand this softness then he will start to understand it. You can be close to it and it seems like he's not going to come through, but if you will keep offering and waiting, why, he will come through. By your recognizing the place and keeping offering, the horse has more of a chance to operate from there. When he once learns to operate from this place of respond and respect, he turns loose then gives. It's something all horses seem to really like. They like to operate from this place.

It doesn't make any difference whether you're stopping, turning around, or backing up—it's the rider recognizing this that makes it work for you.

60

There was either nothing or there was too much. See, you can be right close to it, but the horse, he doesn't recognize it. So you say, "Well, that doesn't work—it isn't getting it," but if you'd just keep waiting and offering it then the meaning starts to come through—the meaning is the horse starting to understand as he starts to feel the same thing you're feeling and understanding. This is where it starts to operate from, but it can feel like it isn't working—it won't work—but it's because he doesn't know how to operate from that. See—that's what makes the difference. It's the human being recognizing what we're talking about—operating from a neutral place. You can be close and nothing coming through because the meaning to the horse isn't there. When he once finds it then he can really operate from there, and he likes it, but the human has to recognize it so that the horse can operate from there.

18. *When a rider is asking a horse to soften and feel back to him and the horse wants to put his head down, what do you do?*

Let him push into it—no different than when he elevates his head. When he elevates his head you just let him push into firmness, too. So if the horse drops way down and pushes into some firmness then he'll come back up to where you want him.

A lot of times a horse will get soft and drop; they call it emptying out. He'll just put his head down on his chest, but if you'll just hold some firmness there, maybe elevate your arms and hands a little, he'll come back up out of there. When he does, then that's the soft feel you're looking for. All you're doing is making the wrong thing difficult and the right thing easy. You're making it difficult for him to drop his head down on his chest and go along; you're making it easy for him to bring his nose, or head, back up and out where you want him to learn to carry it. It's you, the rider, adjusting to fit the situation. Maybe wait and let him find it, let him work his way off it, let him feel his way off it. Don't force him off it and he'll get to where he'll carry his head wherever it's handy for him to carry it and wherever you'd like for him to be. It's no different than elevating his head. If he elevates his head, just go up with him. That will get old and he'll come back down to where you'd like to have it. So you're making the wrong thing difficult and the right thing easy, but you're letting him find it.

The problem, as I take it, is the horse keeps pushing on the rider, so you get the push out by recognizing and rewarding his changes. When he stops pushing there's no pressure. You don't hang on to him when he releases. If he moves up again he moves into pressure again. But he moves into it; you don't pull on him. He'll get so he'll wait for you.

In other words, you're making the wrong things difficult but the right things easy, but you're letting him work at it. You're letting him learn the difference.

It doesn't make any difference how long it takes. It's likely not something you'll be able to correct in five minutes. It depends on your horse—how long he's been doing this. He naturally learns what he has lived. It's always better to be aware and head these things off before they even start. You give the horse a way out by letting him work at it.

This is where a lot of people get disappointed. They want instant results; then if it doesn't come through they think they have to get tougher or rougher. Then they get the horse bothered and upset, and they lose the softness we're looking for. As time goes on and you start to find this place where your horse starts to soften, then you'll get it to carry to a maximum, depending on the horse, how he's understanding it. They are all different, of course. Some horses can really give you a light feel; others are not that sensitive. Each horse can be developed to its own full potential. This is what the rider has to separate.

You feel of him, you feel for him, and you both feel together, but it's something you develop. He learns from one ride to the next. It is complex. When he starts to give, you reward him. Your idea becomes his idea—then you get it to carry—no different from getting a horse to stay put for you at a walk, trot or lope.

You let him work at the wrong things. Don't be afraid or upset if he works at the wrong things. He's learning. That's how we learn something—by working at it—but you try not to drill him on it. There's too much of a variety of things you can try—then a variation of these things to work in, so that he can learn faster and stay put longer.

19. *How do you get a horse to stand when you're saddling it?*

Make the wrong thing difficult and the right thing easy. Let him work at the wrong thing. If he moves off, just bring him back to the same place again. When he wants to stand, then make it easy; first thing you know he'll separate standing still from moving around.

Before a horse moves he gets ready to move, so if you're too far away from him that's an opening for him to move. After he moves you can stop it OK and bring it back. However, another way of making the wrong thing difficult is to observe before he moves, and while he's thinking about it, try just stepping in a few inches or more. It's the little things you do that make a big difference.

Another thing you might try if the horse keeps wanting to drift around is to put him in a bind. Sometimes I'll put one in a bind by taking his head a little shorter. Let him work at it. The first thing you know he'll try to soften up. When he does you let him find it. In other words, when he wants to stop with a soft feel, make sure there is no bind. You'll let him stand, then you'll start again. It may take a while for him to separate the bind from the standing natural, but don't be discouraged or disappointed. Let him work at it.

Your problem may be one of never having the horse gentle enough to begin with. You may have to get him better "sacked out," so to speak, before you even saddle him up. You might have to get him to where he'll accept you around him more. Rub him with your blanket and that sort of thing before you put the saddle on him. Let him work at it. Let him find out the differnece between standing still or having to kind of work at something. The moving off is a "wrong thing" and standing to saddle is the "right thing" in this situation. If he works at it, the horse will find a place to stay put.

Another way to look at the problem of getting a horse to stand while you're saddling up is to think of the way a basketball player uses his body while guarding another player. When you're guarding someone you are there to prevent the other participant from moving. You're there blocking the moves you think he'll try to make. So he has to make a different move. This is the same thing. The horse has to move around you. You're there to block it. He will learn to separate what you want of him. But a lot of times your ball player can get around you; then you fall in behind him and it's too late to do anything about it then. The same way with the horse—you can go to block him but if your timing is off he's already got the start on you. He's already made up his mind to go, whether it is at a walk or a trot— because the person wasn't aware of him getting ready to move or to go, so the person was late. These things make a big difference. When you block something, or guard something, you are on guard yourself to head it off before it starts, if you can. You won't hit on it every time, but if you're aware of it you'll get to where you'll head it off, and then the horse becomes aware of it, too. You've just got that place blocked and the easiest thing for him to do is to stand instead of move away. But he may have to move around quite a bit to find out the difference between being blocked and open. Don't be afraid to let him work at it.

Then, too, while he is trying to understand what you mean he may go through a period when, after you have blocked him, he'll begin to step in towards you instead of away or by you. He could step on your foot or push into you. But if this happens you'll get him to give out away from you. First thing you know you'll get some give; then you'll be able to block it and he'll be staying put.

As you can see, there is a variety of things for the rider to try—always making it easy on the horse to understand.

20. *What kinds of things could you do to keep a horse from rearing?*

The question is how do you keep a horse from rearing. You would get the hindquarters to travel. He gets his weight centered back on his hindquarters. The life comes back to his hindquarters. Some people may use the expression, "the horse is light in the front end." This is when the horse rears. You should get his hindquarters to move one way or the other. Give him someplace to go.

For instance, if you're trying to open a gate, you're trying to get the horse up in a certain place. You may be trying to move him and hold him; this could cause him to want to rear. But you could give him someplace to travel for a little bit, till he understands what you mean. You could move his hindquarters one way or the other, or let him go on by the gate.

If he gets his weight centered back on his hindquarters and you're still holding him a little and pushing him, first thing you know he'll rear. So keep the hindquarters traveling. Get him where you can move the hindquarters one way or the other. Just let him work at the wrong things and make the right things easy.

21. *What kinds of things cause a horse to throw his head?*

He could have some teeth that are sharp and hurt when you take hold of his mouth, or it could be that the head gear is ill fitting. Always check for these things.

If he feels good on his feet he's going to feel good on his head. Any time he's slinging his head, has it upside down, tight and pushing, probably you're not down to his feet. The reason we have reins in our hands and something on his head is to control the life in his body and to control his feet. It could be when you take ahold of him your timing is off and he doesn't understand what he's supposed to do. His out is to sling his head or elevate his head, so he can move his feet. So, it is important that you know where his feet are so that your timing can get right. Then you will be able to move his feet without bothering his head.

To start with, if a horse already has a habit of slinging his head, your timing can be right but he will continue to nod his head or elevate it out of habit. So it can seem like this isn't the answer. But the rider should be patient and fix it up again. If your timing is right, first thing you know the horse will move his feet where they should be, where you are directing them, and his head won't move. It will stay where it should be.

22. *I want a nice free, energetic walk, but all I get is a "nothing feeling." The horse is jigging ahead of my legs with little, hurried steps. His head is tucked way behind the bit with no feel there, either. This happens most frequently leaving for a ride, but during it, too, sometimes. What have I done to cause this? What can I do about it?*

You could be causing some of this by crowding the horse, not feeling the horse prepare to walk fast, not feeling him prepare to come in where he belongs. You feel him after he's into the jigging ahead of your legs or dropped in behind the bit, but that's too late. You need to feel him prepare. You probably aren't noticing the smallest change. You're going by that to get to position.

Now there's prepare and position; it isn't position and prepare. You prepare to get into position. You're trying to get the position without a clear picture of the preparation to get what you want. So you're coming through that and out with this jigging and little hurried steps.

You're probably working too hard at it—not picturing it. I say this because I remember what Tom used to tell me. Tom would come here and work with me and help me, and everything would be great, see. Then he'd be going to leave and I'd say, "Well, I'll work at it!" He'd say, "Don't work too hard," and I'd think, "What does he mean? I've got to work hard at it because I've got to learn it."

Well, I was like you and a lot of other riders. They are working so hard. They are going to make this horse walk or make him do this or that—and I don't mean you've got your teeth bared and you're whippin' and poundin', but you're working so hard to get him to do this or that, you miss feeling him get ready. I know. I went through it.

So, after seven or eight years I said, "To heck with it—it's just not for me." I don't think anyone ever worked any harder at it than I did, believe me. But I finally just said, "It isn't for me!" I just went to riding my horse—just ridin' him. First thing you know I'd think, "Well, I'll be darned! There it is!" Something else would happen, and there it was! I became aware of the little changes. It's not that I have it mastered, but I've been able to get more out of the way to "let it happen."

A rider can't "make it happen," and I'm not referring to physical force—just a make-it-happen attitude can defeat your purpose. Just back off this attitude and *ride the horse* and know where every foot is. Know how it felt when it got there. Know what happened to get it there. First thing you know, you'll get a whole lot more done. You'll back off and let it happen. But it seems like it's something most of us have to go through.

An Interpretation

The Ray Hunt Method of Schooling a Horse

by Vincent W. Carpenter

I attended one of Ray's clinics for five days. They were long days, often ten hours. Some of the following details and sequences may have gaps in them. But Ray's method is based on a philosophy of understanding the horse and yourself. And once you thoroughly understand this philosophy, you can use it in many different ways of your own devising. Therefore this paper is entitled "An Interpretation." Ray doesn't lay out a rigid series of steps. He wants you to figure things out from understanding what a horse is really all about. And, remember, the horse is never wrong, but the rider often is.

INTRODUCTION

All training methods involve some form of physical and visual contact with the horse, from the most brutal beatings to the slightest touch or move. At the one extreme the horse reacts from fear of pain. For instance, the severe bit that a horse reacts to in anticipation of or because of a jab in the mouth. At the other extreme the horse reacts because certain slight touches or movements indicate the rider wants him to do this or that.

Most trainers use methods somewhere in between the two extremes, but veer towards the severe when things don't seem to be progressing. Ray Hunt uses the second extreme almost exclusively, having to rely on pain only very rarely, and then only briefly, usually with a spoiled horse. To break wild mustangs which have rarely seen a human to carry a rider within one day without throwing a fit or bucking seems impossible. Yet the Ray Hunt technique can accomplish it.

THE RAY HUNT THEORY

Ray's theory is based upon a fact which few people realize: an unbroke horse has a fantastic capacity to respect you, respond to you, and become your friend in an incredibly short time span. Most of this is built within the first few hours of teaching. (Ray prefers "teaching" to "training.") And if the wild horse can learn to understand you and be your friend from the very beginning, you can understand why punishment, pain, rope restraints, and fits of bucking are simply not part of a Hunt-taught horse.

How is this fact put to work? Here's how. You put a horse "in a bind," and then *you* give him a "way out." Let *him* find it as his own idea. It is here that the Hunt technique differs dramatically from conventional ones. For instance, you'll rarely if ever see Ray working a horse tied up to a post, or with a foot tied up. Let's say a trainer sacks out a tied-up horse. The horse fights the rope with no way out until he's licked. Or he fights his tied-up foot with no way to put it down, until he's defeated. A Hunt-taught horse is never defeated. He always responds to you because you have made his move his own idea. And he does this amazingly well even at the very beginning of schooling because he notes right away that *you* are the one that gives him a "way out." Therefore *you* become his friend. He learns to trust you.

A BASIC EXAMPLE OF THE THEORY AT WORK

Put an unbroke colt, preferably not even halter-broke, in a small round pen with good high sides. Ray gets in with

70

him. The colt breaks to the other side. Fear. Self-preservation. The colt is tense, hard. Ray moves him around a few times. After the first panic the danger seems a little less, and he stops. Ray approaches. Now starts the process. The colt is in a "bind," being approached by man. He tenses. Ray moves slightly to one side, left. He "opens up" the other side by doing so. This is the signal. The man has given the horse a chance to find his own way out of the bind. The gentlest of all signals, merely visual, no touch. The colt sees the opening and bolts out the open side. Around and around he goes while Ray stands quietly in the middle. Finally he stops again. There. It is all over. The first lesson. The rest of the course consists of hundreds of variations, increasingly subtle, on this same theme.

Ray has a title for the theme. "Make the wrong thing difficult, the right thing easy." ("Wrong" is what you don't want the horse to do; "Right" is what you do want him to do.) In this case Ray stepped a little to the left. He wanted the horse to move to the right. He made it difficult to move to the left, easy to move to the right. And the colt, of his own volition, moved to the open, the right.

O.K. Big deal, you say. Any fool knows a horse would do this. So what? You could do this all day. Where would it get you? It is unbelievable to most people that in these first minutes of work Ray is on the threshold of unlocking a reservoir of friendship, understanding, and respect from the colt, and that he is only minutes away from demonstrating it.

Here is the rest of the session. It might take about a half hour, depending on how nervous the colt is. Ray repeats and repeats the above process. Each time the colt, with a decreasing sense of danger and becoming surer of what he's doing, moves off, always easier and softer, and finally stands.

Now a variation. (Each step in teaching involves secondary goals. In this case the main object is to get the colt used to man, become friendly with him, accept his touch, relax. But at the same time the colt is going to learn to turn easily and naturally at a signal, always towards his new friend, not away from him as if to escape.) The colt stands, either parallel to or facing the fence, with his rump towards Ray. The last we don't need. He would like to leave. Ray approaches. Colt moves around sideways, or even faces Ray. If the latter, first glimmer of understanding. This guy has always given him an opening out of his bind. Not too bad! The variation proceeds. Ray moves slightly in front, maybe lifting the outside hand. Colt is again in a bind, but this time the way out is behind him. He turns hard and finds it. Ray wants that turn towards him, not away. Towards him means acceptance, away means escape. Again repeat and repeat, both left and right. The turns soften, the head and front give, the hindquarters give. Only a relaxed horse is in a mood to learn. Ray can now almost touch the head to bring it around. It gives. The whole body is beginning to give in natural motions to the movements of the teacher. The colt goes less and less distance before standing. When he stops, he faces Ray more often. "This guy isn't so bad. He always gives me a way out." Ray approaches. Colt tenses. Ray tries to pat him in front between the eyes. Colt moves away a bit. Repeated efforts. No luck. Time to loosen him up. Too much standing around getting tense. "This guy has seemed my friend, but now he's trying to touch me." This time as the colt moves away from Ray's attempted touch, Ray slaps him on the rump, and he runs around a bit. Ray keeps him moving, then backs off. Colt stops, facing Ray. This time Ray approaches and is able to rub him lightly on the front of the face.

Time to stop and analyze just what happened here, from the unsuccessful attempt to pat the colt, to the successful. The colt was not doing the "right thing" (standing to be patted), but kept doing the "wrong thing" (moving off). Ray decided it was time to "make the wrong thing difficult." As the colt moved off, Ray *immediately* slapped him on the rump and then kept after him a bit. The timing of the slap, the beginning of making it difficult, should occur *just* as the horse starts to do the wrong thing, so that he can associate them. The "difficult" here is the slap and being run around, because the colt finally decided he would much rather stand and relax with his new-found friend, even if it meant that first touch on the head.

It is time to note one other theme that runs all through Ray's teaching methods: a horse likes to be stroked and patted once he has relaxed and become friendly towards you, and he likes it just about anywhere on his head, body, and legs, contrary to what many horse people believe. Ray proves this time and again, and is continually using it throughout all the lessons to show his gratitude and friendship to horses that are doing the right things.

The rest of this session consists of repetitions of some of the above exercises to reinforce the progress already made. The muscles and moves are getting softer and smoother. The kink in the tail is gone; the ears are working quietly back and forth; the mouth is working; even some sighs—all signs of the colt being more at ease with his new environment.

He is allowed to stand. He turns and faces Ray, takes a few steps toward him and stops out of reach. Ray backs off a few steps (opens the way), and this time the colt walks right up to him for his head rub. (Even my hard-to-catch horse is already responding to this back-away technique.) The colt is now "looking you up," first stages of an easy-to-catch horse. Session over. Maybe 30 to 40 minutes. Not a rope has been used. The groundwork has been laid, and all succeeding lessons are variations on the principles used in this first one.

STARTING AN UNBROKE COLT

Ray emphasizes that, once you thoroughly understand his principles, you can invent your own procedures in teaching a colt. The above section describes just one way you might start him. The clinic I attended had eight colts, four of which were freshly caught from a local wild horse herd. Here are some of the ways he worked them.

Put them all in a round, high corral about 50 feet across. He comes in on his horse, using a 60-foot nylon with a metal honda, ropes one by the neck, takes a dally. Colt breaks to the end of the rope and struggles. The instant he stops, Ray slacks. Makes it easy to stand. He rides up a bit and colt repeats. "Let him find the end of the rope." Repetitions find the colt accepting the rope more and more, stopping and facing Ray more and more. He frequently rides up and makes sure the loop has loosened when he gives slack. Now he wants him to give with a "soft touch" on the rope. He stands his horse about 20 feet away at a slight angle from the colt's facing direction. Puts a slight tension on. Holds it. "His feet are stuck. Come on, boy, you can make it." After a bit the colt softens and moves one foot forward. *Instant* slack. Ray constantly emphasizes "feel and timing" in all stages of teaching and riding a horse. His sense of these is so acute that he often slacks or gives or "makes it easy" for the colt before you can see the animal make a move. The finished product is a horse such as the one Ray is riding, which during this morning session makes thousands of moves in all directions, sideways, backwards, front only, rear only, some just a few slow inches, some an explosive thirty feet. In most instances, try as we spectators would to spot Ray's hand, body, and foot movements, we failed, even though his horse was maneuvering sharply. (I should point out here that this work is not analagous to a cutting horse's unguided moves. Ray's horse awaited his signals for a strategy that changed every few seconds.)

Now, with repetitions, the colt is advancing without hesitation to a soft touch on the rope. You can already see that the "binds" of early teaching become the "signals" (my word) of later teaching. Here, the continual soft tension to get the horse to make his first moves later becomes a brief soft touch, and the colt comes along.

Next Ray shortens up, and has the colt alongside, but facing the opposite direction, the horse and the colt nose to tail. He starts off in a walking circle with the colt on the inside. Colt moves awkwardly backwards parallel to Ray's horse. Hard, tense. "In a bind." His "way out" is to move hindquarters sideways away, front quarters sideways in towards Ray, giving with the head to bend it to the front so he can turn around and walk along with Ray's horse. He softens with repetition and flexibly comes around in either direction. Gets pat on the head. Rubbed all over. Likes it. Ray now with this exercise brings colt's head around with his hand. Rope slack most of the time now. Same goal as when he was on foot with the first colt in the pen. A supple colt giving to a signal, having to separate two moves, giving with the hind before he can come with the front.

At any time about here the colt might be roped around the flanks, and again he finds the end of the line. Getting used to a rope anywhere on his body from the very beginning.

Next Ray puts his loop on a hind foot. (In a few hours these colts become oblivious to a rope anywhere in the air, around their bodies or legs!) Colt storms off. Ray dallies. When the colt quits kicking at the end of the line, he stands, foot in the air. Soon he finds his "way out" by stepping back to get slack and to be able to put his foot on the ground. Repetition. Colt is getting so quiet he has to be moved to get this repetition of coming to the end of the line and stepping back. Ray rides up to colt and puts "soft touch" upwards on roped foot. When it comes, instant slack so the foot returns to the ground. Repetition. Soon foot comes up easily and stays a bit even though it gets slack. Other foot gets same treatment. Colt gets frequent rubs or pats.

Ray calls for the owner to bring the saddle in, put it on

the ground, and approach the colt, still caught by a hind foot. Colt jumps out. Something new. Man on foot approaching. After a fuss he stops. Ray moves behind with slack, out of the picture. After several attempts the owner can approach, rub him on the face, then all over. Ray says, "Pick up a hind foot." He takes up all but a little slack behind the colt and dallies. Owner rubs his way down towards the foot. Colt tightens and lets fly. Ray takes the slack, and the leg is left in the air. Colt backs to put foot on ground. Owner tries again. Sometimes if Ray feels the colt is staying tense, he'll move him around the corral a bit with slack to soften him up. Soon the owner is picking up the feet.

Next he is told to bring up the blanket. He carefully rubs the colt all over with it, and finally flaps it on and off many times. If the colt moves around a bit, he usually stops on his own, Ray keeping slack, "giving him the best deal first." The blanket is on, and next the saddle. Ray says, "Put it on like it's a broke horse." The owner swings it up and on smoothly, off stirrup going over and plunking down on the other side. No problem! And this, the first day! One colt, being appraoched by the owner with the saddle, fidgeted around, and the rider found himself on the off side. Ray said to put it on anyway. Ray's horses will take anything from any direction, if it is done with understanding and "preparation," another key Hunt word.

The saddle is carefully cinched. The colt, always with slack, is sent around the corral a few times, then turned loose into a big open arena. Very few threw more than a couple of halfhearted bucks.

Lesson over, again maybe a half hour, and the rest of the unworked colts are already half used to Ray and his rope, which frequently got wound around some of them in the handling of this first colt.

The clinic I attended lasted five days. The colts were in the mornings, and the owners with saddle horses in the afternoons. The second day the colts got their first ride. First they had to be caught and saddled. Several of them were already "looking up" their owners. Others needed a little help from Ray. With halters on, "soft touch" was applied to the lead ropes. "Patience," Ray repeated. Some colts took several minutes to decide to move, and would get slack the instant a leg stirred forward. A little more, and they finally started to come along. Next came the bridles, all with snaffles. Now the first mounting. Shorten left rein in case he jumps out, and always, always, look for his eye before doing anything. Easy up on the stirrup. Prepare the off side by standing in the stirrup, reaching over the back and rubbing the colt, flapping the right stirrup around a bit. Ray has the colt by a hind foot just in case. Finally the rider is in the saddle. Now move him around the corral pretty good. Off comes the rope. Now Ray really moves him around, the other colts flying out of the way. Slack reins. Out into the big arena.

At last everybody is out on his colt. Use your legs, body, and slap him on the rump to move him out to a trot or lope. No reining. Only a few bucks for some. Others, none. A critical time now in the teaching. The colts have, in two days, entered a new world of gentle friendship with their owners. And many of them want to keep it this way, which means they would just like to stand around or poke along at a slow walk. They must learn right now that whenever their rider is up, they must be constantly alert, ready to move out. So, keep those colts part of the time moving briskly during this formative stage. But the second one breaks into a quicker movement, stop whatever you were doing to get him there, just as you slacked the lead rope the instant he responded to your slight tension. He'll usually back off again right away, which is fine. Repeat and repeat. Then let him relax a while in a walk or stand.

The rest of the days were more of the same, with the addition of sacking, reining, rides out into the hills, and swinging ropes off the colt.

First each rider was given a sack, which he carefully rubbed all over the colt. Then he mounted, rode around, rubbing the colt some more, finally using the sack as an aid to getting into a trot or lope. Soon sacks were waving all over the place and slapping the colts on all sides.

The first stages of reining involved getting the colt to "give" his head. This point was stressed repeatedly early on. If the colt ran off with you, and he had been taught to give his head, you could get him back in control. Remember, he had already had some practice at this when Ray was working him on his horse. The rider stands his colt, then takes one rein wide with a soft touch, leaving the other slack. After a moment the head comes around and immediately gets a nice pat. Repetition of this on both sides during the remainder of the week. Ray wasn't satisfied until the head came way around towards the rider. It wasn't long before they were bending easily to receive their rubs. And from here to turning was a short step, always plow-reining with a soft touch. "Wait for his legs to come," rang out all week long. "Feel and understanding." You don't "job" a horse around. When he responds and starts to turn at your touch, you feel his legs change and go with him. You don't pull the rein and lean out as if to say, *"You* come with *me."* Let your idea become his idea.

Now Ray opened the gate, and off they all went for a ride into the hills.

A later stage of teaching finds Ray out in the arena on foot, carrying a piece of stiff wire with a flag on the end of it. He has a rider start to turn his colt from a stand. Just as he does so, Ray steps slightly to the outside of the turn and flaps his flag. The colt's front legs come off the ground, he pivots around his hind feet and does his first offset. Here, as

78

well as at many other stages, the colt is learning to separate
the increasing number of different signals he's getting. If he
gets confused, it's the rider's fault. "Patience and understanding," Ray admonishes. In this case, the colt is now
learning to give with his hindquarters ("Feel those hind
legs reach out sideways") when you bring the inside rein
hand to your chest, leaving the outside rein slack. And
moving his front end around sideways when you take the
inside rein hand out wide and support it with the outside
rein lightly on the colt's neck. These moves are practiced
separately, so the colt can learn the difference. Then, for
these first offsets, the hindquarters are signaled to be
moved. Just as they do so, the rider signals the front
around, and gets an assist from Ray's flag.

Later the rider reaches out with a soft touch for both
reins. Time to learn collection and stops. These colts will
soon be stopping head down, nose tucked, on a light rein,
never veering from a straight-ahead direction.

Finally, the last day, the riders carry their ropes and
gradually work them until the colts accept the loops all
over, underneath, and around their feet.

THE EQUITATION CLASSES

Ray was candid about his preference for the colt classes
over the afternoon classes with us. The reasons were clear.
The colts were untouched when started, and the results
were dramatic. Our older horses, trained (or untrained) in a
variety of ways, were "calloused" and, in some cases,
spoiled. Yet, all of us saw evidence of progress during the
week, sometimes amazing progress.

We practiced the basics over and over. Walk, trot, lope,
stop, back. In straight lines, circles, and figure eights, using
the same principles we learned by observing the colts,
always with a rein in each hand. Getting the horse to stand
and give his head for a rub. Stops always collected. Fastest
walk possible. Slowest. Feel the life in his body. "From

79

your mind, through your body, to the horse's body." "Wait for his feet to come." Make those circles perfect with no change in his action from entering to leaving them. The horse's body, from nose to tail, should give and fit the curve of his circle perfectly. Walk ahead ten steps, then back three. Try to keep the life in his body so the move from ahead to reverse is one fluid motion. Soft touch always. Back in circles. Know where his feet are at all times. You can't offset or change leads correctly if you signal him with the wrong foot on the ground. We'd have to walk or trot by Ray, counting cadence to a given foot from the feel of the horse.

Use your body, feet, reins, "whatever you have to do." Ray, unlike many teachers, was never very specific about such things as leg aids. Sure, use them (sparingly, as with all your signals), but *you* figure out what to do with your legs. You know Ray's principles well enough by now. However, if a rider was really puzzled about something, he was given ample opportunity to pin Ray down about specific moves or pressures.

A few comments about a horse learning to separate things out for himself. We were shown that, at a stand, by "reaching for the reins with a soft touch" (translates into: shorten up on your reins and come back with a slight tension), we could do one of three things: lower the horse's head till it touched the ground; collect his head; back. To lower it to the ground, reach and give each time he lowers until it's all the way down. To collect, reach and maintain a soft touch, using a little leg pressure to keep him from backing. To back, reach and give when he backs (obviously, on paper, the same signal used to put his head on the ground). There has to be a little something extra from the rider to allow the horse to separate these three out, since they all involve a little tension on both reins. I found myself totally confusing my horse. This was not helped by the fact that she never had a day of real schooling in her life, knows nothing but cow work, and had always backed (sort of) on a heavy rein with a curb bit. (I'm back to a snaffle now.) All week long we periodically practiced each of the above moves. I stubbornly refused to use any more than a soft touch. ("Soft," for Ray, meant the equivalent of draping the two reins over one finger and moving it back!) In trying to back, often nothing would happen, or the head would start lowering to the ground. Sometimes I'd get a step or two back. Ray had already spoken several times, but it hadn't sunk in. "Do what you have to do." Typically, he never commented on my failures. Let me figure it out. He's told me enough by this time, I should know better. Finally the last day, when we were asked to back in quarter and half circles, I could stand it no longer and went back to the heavy pressure on the reins the mare was used to. Success. Back to the soft touch. Occasional success. Now a little harder, then even softer. More success. It struck me that I had had her so confused, I'd forget collection and head lowering and just concentrate on backing, my next several times on her. It's been working. Now I've returned to collection. She, and I, are learning to separate these, and always with a softer touch.

A couple of cases of spoiled horses. One was mine. She is sensitive, responsive, a little wild, a streak of her ancestry, perhaps (she was caught out of a wild herd, too). A few years ago you could pick up her feet. Then on a few occasions I asked some of the boys at the ranch to trim them. One time they couldn't catch her in the corral, and she jumped clean out. Another time she threw a 240-pound man who was working on one of her hind legs about 40 feet. After that nobody could touch the hind end. Ray put her in the corral, haltered, not tied up. (No claustrophobia for his horses.) He rubbed her over and picked up the front feet. Worked his way back. Down the hind leg, and off she moved. Caught her eye again. Lead rope with slack in his left hand on her hip (so she couldn't jump ahead and kick

81

him), his right hand caressed its way down the leg again. Failure. Repeated from the front end. Then back again. No go. Here came the old theme once more. She was doing the wrong thing. Make it difficult. *Just* as she moved off that time, she got a slap on the rump plus about ten seconds of shooing around the corral, jumping and snorting. Ray quit. She quit. She would much rather have stood and got patted than got spooked around. Next time he picked up the foot, but again she moved away. Repeat of the "difficult," but less. Next time he got the foot up and gave it back to her without her moving. Rubbed the leg. He picked it up and rested it on his knees. (He gave it back to her all right, but in a new position. "Preparation" for what was coming.) Picked it up and worked leg back and forth. Tense. More rubs. Soon the leg was soft and gave. Finally back to the shoeing position. Then the other side. Elapsed time: ten minutes. Back here at the ranch I get off, drop the reins, and pick those feet up. The boys are incredulous.

One more illustration. This was a horse that really blew his stack trailer loading. They backed a four place stock trailer into a dip on the ground so the floor was ground level. The owner led the horse up, flicked the lead rope gently, quitting whenever the horse stepped closer. During the next ten minutes the horse actually loaded a few times. But Ray could see the horse wasn't totally convinced. He insisted on more loading. Sure enough, no more success. Rearing and balking. A half hour passed and the poor girl was getting arm weary, as she had been told to increase the pressure. Ray then took the horse, put on a war bridle with his nylon, and continued where the girl left off. "The best deal first." Little flicks on the rope, with instant slack each time the horse moved closer. Suddenly he balked and started to turn away. Immediately a hard jerk. The loop around the nose snapped tight, and the horse reared in surprise. Two more hard jerks where he was still in the air, and he came down blowing and tense. Instant slack. Let him think over what happened. More soft touches. Again approach. Again turn away with an immediate jerk on the rope. Slack. More flicks, and he loads. Instant slack. Nervously backs out. Dozens of repeats. Always softer. Doesn't unload now till he feels a little touch on the rope. Now Ray wants him all the way to the front. Two feet to go. He commences little slaps with his coil on the rump. A move forward and he quits the slaps. One foot to go. Works with the coil again, and finally the horse is all the way to the front. Repeats. Stops him half way in, stops him half way out. The flicks are no longer needed. He is fully loaded and unloaded on a loose rope. Next a two horse trailer. Repeats. Horse quiet and relaxed. Ten, fifteen times. Elapsed time (including girl's work): one hour.

CONCLUSION

First of all I apologize for the multitude of repetitions in this paper. The clinic was full of repetitions. It had to be. The key words and key philosophy are so disarmingly simple, they have to be drummed into the horseman until their full significance becomes a part of his every thought and move.

Finally, the advantages of the Ray Hunt method. Number one, you have a quiet, calm horse. So calm, in fact, that once when Ray took one of his own horses to a national sale where they were displaying reining, he didn't get a bid the first day in spite of a flawless performance. He found out the buyers thought his horse was drugged! The second day, another flawless performance, and the buyers gradually realized the horse was always this way. The bids started coming and went on up to a healthy sum.

Number two. Speed and ease of training. When you describe the Hunt method to other trainers, they say, "Sure, that's fine, if you want to spend all year breaking a horse." Then some of them attend a clinic, and they have been observed walking away, muttering to themselves in disbelief at what they have seen. Remember, Ray had eight colts to work for five half days, plus lots of time spent lecturing to all the students and helping get them started. If he had had just one colt by himself, the time span would have been hours, not days. Conventional training methods allow you to spend only short periods with young, unbroke colts. Ray's method of having your idea become the colt's idea greatly lengthens the periods before the colt becomes tired and inattentive.

And, to close, number three. Since you have a horse whose every move is ultimately his own idea, every move is completely natural, just as if he were out in the pasture playing with some other horses, therefore done with maximum efficiency, ease, and stability.

Equesology

There's a purpose and a meaning behind each thing you ask the horse to do.

Make the wrong things difficult, and the right things easy.

If you are going to teach a horse something and have a good relationship, you don't make him learn it—you let him learn it.

The horse learns not to be particular if the rider is not particular.

Think right down to the ground.

Instead of a hard tightness, try to find a soft firmness.

You don't pull on the horse; he pulls on you—there's a big difference.

Don't be afraid to expose your horse to something he hasn't quite been exposed to yet, but don't snow him under.

The feet are in your hands.

The right feel and timing bring you the balance.

Get the feet soft and they'll be soft in the head.

The slower you do it the quicker you'll find it—it can happen so soon you don't feel it.

THINK

Prepare ahead of time.
> *Let them learn—let them work at it.*
> *Let your horse be a winner.*
> *Let your horse be proud.*

Ride your horse with your whole body, not just with your arms and legs.

Your arms and body are working in rhythm with his feet and legs.

You are with him every stride.

If you haven't got his attention you don't try to direct it.

You don't change; you just add on—work it in with what you're doing.

Watch the gauges just like the indicators in the car—watch his ears—watch his eyes; they are good indicators.

Notice the smallest change and the slightest try and reward him.

There's a difference between firm and hard—you may have to get firm but don't get hard with your arms and hands.

You want your horse soft but not lazy.

The rider should stay alive and stay alert.

Let your idea become the horse's idea.

Your horse is not your slave—he's your partner.

Try to keep his mind soft and mellow.

Ride with life in your body.

If you're happy, your horse is more apt to be happy.

Admire the horse for the good things he does and just kinda ignore the wrong things. First thing you know, the good things will get better and the bad things will get less.

You can't teach experience.

He knows that you know and you know he knows.

Adjust to fit the situation.

You're not working on the horse, you're working on yourself.

You've got to be one mind and one body.